W9-BLU-583

CONSCIOUS LIVING

ALSO BY GAY HENDRICKS

Conscious Loving (with Kathlyn Hendricks)

Learning to Love Yourself

At the Speed of Life

Conscious Breathing

The Corporate Mystic (with Kate Ludeman)

The Conscious Heart (with Kathlyn Hendricks)

A Year of Living Consciously

CONSCIOUS LIVING

FINDING JOY IN THE REAL WORLD

GAY HENDRICKS, PH.D.

HarperSanFrancisco
A Division of HarperCollins*Publishers*

 For information address HarperCollins Publishers, Inc., 10 East 53rd Street, New York, NY 10022.

HarperCollins books may be purchased for educational, business, or sales promotional use. For information please write: Special Markets Department, HarperCollins Publishers, Inc., 10 East 53rd Street, New York, NY 10022.

HarperCollins Web site: http://www.harpercollins.com

FIRST EDITION

Designed by Kris Tobiassen

Library of Congress Cataloging-in-Publication Data

Hendricks, Gay.
Conscious living : finding joy in the real world / Gay Hendricks. — 1st ed.
p. cm.
ISBN 0-06-251488-1 (cloth)
ISBN 0-06-251487-3 (pbk.)
1. Conduct of life. I. Title.
BF637.C5H47 2000
158—dc21 99-37275

---

00 01 02 03 04 RRD(H) 10 9 8 7 6 5 4 3 2 1

With deep gratitude, I dedicate this book to two people whose passion and commitment set the standard I aim for every day:

KATHLYN THATCHER HENDRICKS—
wife, creative partner, and boon companion

and

DAVID HUBBARD—
consummate truthseeker and treasured friend of three decades.

Both of you have shared, in person or in my mind, every crucial conversation that inspired this book. When I discovered the following poem of Rilke's, I thought of you both and translated it anew in your honor.

The one who grasps the thousand contradictions of his life integrates them into a single whole,
that man, joyous and grateful, drives the hooligans out of the mansion, celebrates in a different way, and you are the guest he welcomes in the still of the evening.
You are the second person in his quiet space, the still center of his conversations with himself; and every circle he draws around you raises him out of time on the legs of a compass.

—RAINER MARIA RILKE

Contents

Acknowledgments

I am deeply grateful to the many friends, students, and colleagues who have helped shape my work over the past three decades.

In the early days, I was guided by the warm hearts and fine minds of Dwight Webb, John Krumboltz, Carl Thoresen, and Steven Zifferblatt. During my years at the University of Colorado, I benefited from many stimulating conversations with Barry Weinhold, Dennis Mithaug, and David Fenell. In recent years, as my emphasis has shifted toward disseminating the ideas of conscious living and loving to the entertainment world, I have been deeply enriched by the brilliant insights and warm hospitality of Kenny and Julia Loggins. Gary Zukav, Jack Canfield, and Bonnie Raitt have given me the benefit of their life wisdom and learning and have broadened my thinking immeasurably. The friendships of Marilyn Tam, Jerry and Carole Isenberg, Christen Brown, Orson Mozes, Buddy Winston, Steve Simon, and Catherine Miller have provided a heartfelt space in which I can feel at home wherever I am in the world.

I also wish to honor the memories of my beloved grandmother, Rebecca Delle Canaday, and my mother, Norma Canaday

Hendricks, whose remarkable gifts and eccentric ways mean more to me every day. In my living family, I appreciate the quick mind and brilliant writing talents of my niece and frequent coauthor, Laura Joyce, and the steadfast loyalty of other members, including my brother, Mike, and his wife, Lou Ann.

There are many others, too numerous to name, but you know who you are and how deeply you live in my heart.

Introduction

A Personal Journey to a Conscious Life

Eternity is a child at play with colored balls.

HERACLITUS, FRAGMENT 53

In my early thirties I made a discovery about love that changed everything about my life. The discovery enabled me to attain my heart's deepest yearning: a lasting love relationship rich with happiness and creativity.

The realization was this: the only way to attract the love you want is to love and embrace your *self.* For years, through many unsatisfying relationships, I had been trapped inside the bubble of a delusion. I was trying to get other people to love me deeply and unconditionally, but without ever having loved my *self* unconditionally. In retrospect, it seems obvious, but at the time it was anything but. Right after having this realization, I put it into action.

I let go of my defenses and relaxed into a few seconds of pure, loving acceptance for all of myself. I loved and accepted my anger, my fear, my loneliness, and all the other things I didn't like about myself. I even loved myself for not being able to love myself very well! I could do it only for an instant at first, but these few seconds of unconditional love for my self changed my whole approach to life. Ultimately I resigned from the exhausting task of seeking love outside myself to complete myself.

In time this realization led me to see that my job now was to be a producer and distributor of love, not a consumer! I dropped the restless, mindless search for love in all the wrong places. In fact, I dropped the search for love *anywhere* outside myself. Instead, I began to look for the places in me that needed loving.

This inner shift caused real magic to happen immediately in my outer life. Suddenly a woman appeared in my life—as if by magic—and she was exactly the kind of person I'd always dreamed of.

There was a very good reason I'd never found her before. Unconsciously I had been looking for a woman to complete me and make me whole through the power of her love. Suddenly I realized that it was my job to complete myself through *my* power of loving me. From this place of wholeness, I would naturally attract another whole person who loved herself to exactly the degree I did. Then our lives together could become a journey of two whole people celebrating each other and ourselves. When problems and barriers emerged in our relationship—as they surely would—we would work through those barriers as two allies committed to our mutual development.

And that's just what happened.

The past twenty years with Kathlyn have been exactly that kind of magical journey. Two kids, nine coauthored books, five hundred radio and television interviews, and thirty-some trips around the world later, I can report that the magic is real and sustainable. I never imagined how good it could get. I now know that it's possible to live and learn and even work together through twenty years of creative harmony.

The love we all seek is right here, right now. A simple shift of consciousness, and the floodgates open. This book is about how to make the shift to a new kind of conscious living and loving. If you read Kathlyn's and my earlier book, *Conscious Loving*, you will find that the book you're holding complements the previous work but goes into a new dimension: the transformation of your inner self. I've come to believe that the process of learning to live consciously begins in the depths of our inner selves. This book—particularly part 1—is directed at you and your relationship with yourself. In part 2 I will discuss relationships with others, but with particular focus on what I've learned in the decade after *Conscious Loving* was published.

This book takes a larger perspective than my previous work. The journey of conscious *loving* is part of a larger path of conscious *living*. In a very real sense, conscious loving is something you do in every moment of living, whether it comes to life in the way you grip your steering wheel in heavy traffic or the way you embrace your beloved in breathless ecstasy. It's all the same thing! The very same discoveries that brought a rich love relationship into my life could also be applied to creating a life rich in creativity, good feeling, and even financial abundance.

My Personal Journey of Conscious Living

"Where could you have possibly come from?"

As a child I heard this question often, and it was usually uttered in tones of exasperation. Now that the sting has worn off, I wonder about it myself. The differences between my family members and me could go on for pages:

I like chocolate; everybody else in my family hated it.
I'm the lone mystic in a family of hardheaded skeptics.
I write books about relationship, psychology, and spirituality; no one in my family has ever read one of them or even acknowledged gift copies I sent.

My brother often goes to Scotland and France on one sort of spirit quest: he tours the great distilleries and vintners in search of the perfect sip. My spirit quest has taken me to monasteries in India, Tibet, and Nepal, to grand cathedrals, humble caves, and epic shamanic journeys in the outback of Mexico. Even thinking of whiskey gives me an inner cringe; I may be one of the few people this side of Utah who's never been drunk or even managed to finish a whole beer.

You get the picture. Even after I had published a dozen books and was a tenured professor at a major university, my mother would still ask me occasionally if I ever planned to get a real job. Finally, an appearance on *Oprah* seemed to convince members of my family that I wasn't in a fly-by-night profession after all!

Many of us begin the journey so that we can find a way through the frequently awful life situations we find ourselves in. That was certainly true for me. Part of my quest was inspired by a search for survival tools to use on myself. As I looked around while I was growing up, almost no one seemed happy. Most everyone wore downward-pulling mouths and deep worry grooves on their foreheads. Addictions were rampant. Family photos reveal that I adopted these masks myself by the time I was in high school. Pictures in my late teens and early twenties show me with a much more wrinkled brow than I have now. The wrinkles disappeared after a great awakening in my early twenties that I will soon describe, and fortunately they haven't come back.

The pain on the faces of the married couples in my family troubled me deeply as a child. Even now, as I pause to look at old family photos, I find it hard to look without flinching. In your imagination, look over my shoulder as I hold a family photo in my hand. It is a photograph of my grandparents at their fiftieth wedding anniversary. I was there and remember the day vividly. It took hours to get the picture, because they were unwilling to sit on the same piece of furniture to have the picture snapped. Sitting on the couch together would indicate a degree of intimacy that they did not wish to communicate to posterity. A compromise was reached only after a lengthy and bitter negotiation. My grandfather agreed to occupy the seat of the couch, while my grandmother would only perch on the armrest at the other end. This solution allowed them both to be right. The portrait reveals my grandfather looking helpless and confused as he stares blankly at the camera with his mouth agape, while my grandmother looks off in the other direction, her jaw set in silent rage.

They had a terribly strained relationship, and my inquiries have revealed that it was like this throughout most of the sixty years they were married. My brother once asked my grandmother why things were so difficult between her and my grandfather. She reflected a moment, then said, "I think it's because I hated him from the moment I met him." That explained it to my satisfaction.

My young mind was always wondering, how can they be so unhappy? These were wonderful people when they were out of each other's range. They fed and clothed me, showered me with love, and probably saved my life. I felt so sad that they could not be civil to each other even on special occasions. What had gone wrong between them? What would it take to bring serenity and happiness back into their pinched faces?

I felt a passionate sense of mission to figure out what had created that degree of pain. I wanted to avoid creating anything like it in my own relationships. But try as I might, my unconscious programming caught up with me, thrusting me first into a backlash. By my teen years, I was so bitter on the subject that I wrote an essay called "Marriage" in the ninth or tenth grade. I had completely forgotten it until my niece discovered it in an attic and sent it to me when I was about forty-five years old. The first line says it all: "There are very few things about which I am absolutely certain, but the one thing I am completely certain about is that I will never, ever get married." After taking this position, I swung to the opposite extreme in my early twenties. I not only got married, but my marriage unfolded as an uncanny replay of the worst of my family scripts. Fortunately, I got a second chance.

Questions Are Powerful Magic

In nearly thirty years of teaching and therapy, I've made the following recommendation more than any other: figure out the questions that you, with all your heart and soul, most need to ask. Don't worry about the answers. Put your attention on the questions themselves, and keep going for deeper and deeper questions until you come to the one or two or three that your life purpose is centered around. As the poet Rilke put it, "Learn to love the questions themselves." The magic is this: if you ask your big questions with sincerity and all your heart, your life itself will become a living answer to them.

There is another reason that questions are powerful medicine. If your question is vast and deeply personal and you really don't know the answer to it, you set the stage for previously unthinkable leaps of consciousness. If you open up to genuine wonder, you step out of the zone of the known and into the infinite creative possibilities of the unknown.

An Early Leap and a Resounding Thud

My childhood interests in matters of the heart and soul set the stage for a profound peak experience and an equally profound fall from grace. Both were essential to my growth, and both occurred around the time I entered elementary school.

I was playing in the side yard by myself one afternoon, probably a month or two before I would begin elementary school. I had been attending vacation Bible school at the church my family belonged to. There had been many stories about Jesus being the son of God, and I was trying to figure out what all this meant.

I remember that it was a hot and muggy day, even by Florida standards, and that I had just taken my shirt off. I suddenly felt a call to pause and rest for a moment. A question gripped my mind: was I, too, a son of God? It seemed possible, because I had no father in my life. Where had I come from? Was that invisible father in the sky my real father? I looked up through the oak branches to the shimmering sky beyond, and an awareness came over me.

"I am made of the same stuff as everything else in the world. I am the same as the oak leaf and the earthworm and the sky beyond. It is all one thing, and I am a part of it."

In that moment I knew that all humans are connected to one another and all are exactly the same, even though we come in different packages. I saw that I was made of the same stuff as my mother and my brother and my Uncle Marlow, even though we each had very different personalities.

Of course, I lacked the vocabulary to state the idea coherently, but I remember the feeling as if it happened ten minutes ago: There is a Oneness. We have it inside us, and it has us inside it.

The feeling soothed me deeply. I remember feeling a great sense of peace after it happened. I felt secure knowing that I was all of a piece and so was everything else. I had no idea the same idea had been occurring to people throughout history.

Nearly forty years later I opened a book written two thousand years ago by Marcus Aurelius, then living in a military outpost while defending Rome against the barbarians. This wise and heartfelt man kept a journal that he called "To Himself" and that we now call *The Meditations of Marcus Aurelius.* It consists of twelve notebooks, and in the tenth one he writes,

> Let us agree on this first: I am part of the whole, all of which is governed by nature. Next, let us agree on this: I am intimately related to the parts which are the same kind as myself. If I remember these two things, I cannot be discontented with anything that arises out of the whole, because I am connected to the whole. Nothing that comes out of the whole can injure a part, because nature cannot generate anything harmful to itself. In remembering, then, that I am a part of the whole, I shall be content with everything that happens.

It is basically the same idea that appeared spontaneously in the heart and mind of a youngster in the early 1950s, in the swamplands of Florida.

Where could this notion have sprung from? Is it part of our heritage, somehow encoded in our bodies and minds? Is it something we can feel again and again? It would take me a long time to find out, because I came down out of this exaltation with a thud: I entered the first grade.

At first I was very excited to be entering school. There would be other kids to play with and something new to learn every day! My brother, Mike, who was starting junior high school as I entered first grade, had told me there was a subject called social studies. I made up my own fantasies about the content. It would be a time every day when we would learn how to solve problems in our lives and our families. We would learn the skills of how to conduct a social life—how to talk to people without being afraid, how to ask adults things without getting them upset. Boy, was I wrong! Social studies turned out to be learning things like the major exports of Bolivia. But the curriculum wasn't the only problem. I was a problem myself, and I remember the shock of finding it out.

When I entered school, I found out something I had not known before: I was a family problem. In my early years I was raised primarily by my grandparents. My grandparents doted on me; even though they didn't get along with each other, they were totally loving and endlessly patient with me. I had no way of knowing that I had something wrong with me, because I was always in the radiant field of my grandparents' caring. To explain why and how I was a problem, let me introduce my mother.

In 1933 my mother, Norma Canaday, married her dream man, Leonard Gay Hendricks. She was a great planner, and her plan was this: she would work at an office job until she had the one child she wanted, then she would quit the job and be a housewife and writer until she attained her dream of publishing the Great Southern Novel. My father would support the small family with his job as manager of a factory a few blocks from their house.

The desired son was born in 1937, and other elements of the plan were in place, when life intervened harshly and abruptly one day in 1944. The war had not disrupted her life very much, mainly because my father was 4-F for being obese and having flat feet (the same conditions that kept me from slogging around the jungles of Vietnam when I was drafted in 1967). It had, however, forced her to keep working part-time, so she had postponed her writing career until her son entered school. With the newfound freedom, she would launch her writing career.

Now for the hard part. One day my father, lunch box in hand, walked off to work and never came home. He became ill that day and had to be rushed to the hospital. No one knows exactly what the problem was, but something caused his kidneys to fail rapidly. Within a week he developed uremic poisoning, and he died at age thirty-two. My mother was grief-stricken, but she mobilized all her strength and pushed through the bereavement, the funeral, and the unpleasant surprise of discovering she had been left nearly penniless. My father, known for his new cars, his natty wardrobe, and his generosity to friends, had borrowed against his life insurance so much that after funeral expenses my mother was left with less than three hundred dollars to her name.

Now for the harder part. A few months after the funeral, the stress was still so great she was practically living on coffee and cigarettes. Always slender, she had lost thirty pounds and now carried less than one hundred pounds on her 5'10" frame. One day it occurred to her that she had not had a period since the funeral. At first she attributed it to stress, but a visit to the doctor proved otherwise. She had conceived a child, probably only a few weeks before the funeral. At this news, her steely composure broke, and she sank into despair.

Fortunately, she lived in the midst of an extended family, which, though poor and emotionally reserved, rallied around her until she got her feet back on the ground. Practically force-fed by my grandmother, my mother finally topped the hundred-pound mark and began to regain health. In the fall of 1944, she put her six-year-old son in school and sat back, not to pursue her writing career, but to await the birth of her second son.

That was me.

From the very beginning I was fat. Pictures show me with roll upon roll of fat on my arms and legs. By the end of six months I weighed more than most babies at one year. Various theories were advanced: Perhaps my mother's semistarvation had jiggered some inner thermostat so that now I stored fat more readily. Perhaps I had inherited my father's and grandmother's thyroid problem. Perhaps I would outgrow it.

But I knew nothing of this. My grandparents took over primary care for me, because my mother had her hands full looking for a job, raising Mike, and trying to stay above water. My grandmother was sixty-five and my grandfather sixty-eight when I was born. I am deeply grateful that they were willing to take me in at a time when they would normally have been gardening, working crossword puzzles, and doing other things they loved to do.

In their presence there was never a harsh word about me or to me, in sharp contrast to the volatile hours I spent at my mother's house. At my grandparents' my days were occupied with playing by myself, having stories read to me, learning card games from my grandfather, and accompanying him to the baseball park where he was the groundskeeper. I spent a lot of time alone and even taught myself to read so I could amuse myself better. According to my aunt, an elementary teacher, I could already read at the third-grade level when I entered school. Pictures from that time show me as radiantly happy (and very fat).

Then I went to school.

Unknown to me, my weight problems had been an ongoing focus of concern, the Family Problem. I had no idea of this and did not even know I was fat. I had no external reference to compare myself to. I was just who I was. When I entered elementary school, I suddenly became aware of my different status. I was taunted with names like "Fatty" and "Pork Chop." Kids had a field day punching me and running away, because they knew I couldn't catch them. On one of my first school days I tried unsuccessfully to climb a jungle gym, slipped, and broke my nose. I came home and demanded, "Am I fat? Is there something wrong with me?"

I felt bewildered and hurt, betrayed and doomed. It had never occurred to me that there was anything wrong with me. Now, not only did I know it, but I knew everyone else had known it all along. They just hadn't told me. I felt heartsick, but I took a secret vow never to tell anyone how I felt.

I built a workable persona on top of all this pain. Nowadays I call this persona the Little Professor; back then I just focused all my energy on knowing everything there was to know and proving to my teachers I knew it. By the time I finished first grade I had already done all the second grade work and then some. I leapfrogged directly into third grade, and there I hit another wall.

I had never realized it, and certainly didn't understand it, but I used my eyes for another purpose besides seeing the usual visual spectrum. I could see streams of energy around me and other people, and I used seeing the energy streams for my survival. The skill became crucial to my well-being, because by then I had left the safety zone of my grandparents' house and was living with my mother. I could see when my mother was about to blow up by watching the intensity of the vibrations. By doing this, I could disappear from the scene before the storm hit. My brother was not skilled at this, and often he bore the brunt of the tirade by simply being in the wrong place at the wrong time.

Everything changed one day when an optometrist came to my classroom. An eye test revealed that one of my eyes didn't work very well, while the other eye saw perfectly. I was outfitted with a clunky black pair of glasses, the type worn by a popular jazz musician of the era, Dave Brubeck. I looked ridiculous, but worse, my ability to see energy streams disappeared. Now, not only was I fat, but I had lost my secret vision. From then on, I slid further into despair. By the time I was in junior high school, I was a hundred pounds overweight and was making C's and D's.

Imagine a river that disappears under desert sands, only to reemerge on the other side. That's how my adolescence seems to me now. There must have been a river flowing down underneath somewhere, but I was not in touch with it. I don't remember having any further insights or spiritual experiences until the stream broke through in a most unusual way in my early twenties. Looking back, I think I was simply on autopilot.

I got a reprieve from the prison of obesity when I was in the ninth grade. I was sent to a weight specialist in Valdosta, Georgia, a doctor named E. C. Jungck (I remember the name because it was written on many pill bottles in the medicine cabinet). He put me on a severe diet and an array of diet pills. I lost a lot of weight and jumped to straight A's in school, boosted by the heart-pounding and mind-perking properties of the amphetamines that were the core of Dr. Jungck's program. Through exercise, I kept the weight off until college, but it eventually returned. By my early twenties I had regained the hundred pounds. Fortunately, I stumbled upon a permanent solution—emphasis on stumble—of which you will hear more shortly. (This morning I weighed 179—still no Mick Jagger or Baryshnikov—but with my 6'1" frame I now resemble a fullback more than a sumo wrestler.)

The saving grace of my adolescence was a profound relationship with a wonderful young woman named Alice, whom I met when I was sixteen. My love for her felt like a once-in-a-lifetime thing, and I assumed we would always be together. The thought that I might love any other person, or that she might, never crossed my mind. This was it. We were together for the last part of high school and the first two years of college. But one day, late in my sophomore year, Alice asked me to meet her for a talk. She said there was too huge a gap between the "real me" and the outer self I presented to the world. She said she loved the inner me but had stopped liking my outer persona. I pressed her for more, and she admitted that she had fallen in love with another man. Later I met him, and I could see why. He looked like a Greek god, with flowing blond hair and an athletic body. He was carrying a book of T. S. Eliot poems and a volume by someone named Jung. I was heartbroken and angry, but after the anger began to dissipate, I compared myself to him and came up with a sobering realization: what woman in her right mind would choose me over someone like him? I was fat, could never figure out what Eliot's poems meant, and had never heard of Jung.

This loss hit me hard, but a far worse one followed soon. My grandmother had a stroke, and my memory of the next year becomes a blur. One moment I was at her hospital bedside, watching her labored breathing assisted by life support. The next moment I can recall, my family was conferring about whether to turn off the machinery. She was in a coma, and there was no electrical activity in her brain. I must have sounded like a little boy instead of a bulky adult, because I remember stammering something like, "Hold on, this can't be happening. You mean she's not going to be all right?" I had grown up with the secure knowledge of her invincibility, and I don't think it had ever occurred to me she might die. My aunt Audrey and my mother looked at me like I was crazy. No, they said. This is it. She's not coming back.

Because I was so out of touch with my feelings, I did not know how to grieve. I lived in denial of the loss of my grandmother and Alice. I tried not to think about them and never spoke a word about my feelings to anyone. Predictably, my life became a 3-D movie of the unclaimed feelings and issues in my unconscious.

I made a desperate and unconscious search for a security blanket, and within months of my grandmother's death, I became attached to a woman who was exactly like me. She was deeply wounded by early losses, and she had built a thick wall around them. She had a charming outer act, totally false, like mine, and inside she smoldered, like me, with awesome rage and grief. She, too, had lost her father, her grandmother, and her first love but had covered all of it over with a pert cheerleader persona. She also had a substance addiction I did not discover until after we were married.

I'm not sure if we were a match made in heaven or hell, but we spent most of our time in the latter. Our wedding was the union of two false fronts. We had little idea who we were as individuals, and we had less insight into who the other person was. Within days of the wedding our outer masks cracked and torrents of ancient pain poured out—misdirected at each other. Now, looking back from the safe perspective of thirty years' distance and insight, I can think of only one other relationship to compare it to—my grandparents'. It was the only marriage I witnessed close-up in my early years, and I believe that I made an inner movie of it in my unconscious. Later I would base my first marriage on this script. As I write this I feel myself shuddering as I recall how deeply asleep I was throughout this period of my life. But then, through luck or grace or the sheer force of a lifestream flowing beneath the desert of my life, I received a second chance.

A Moment That Changed My World

Hands thrust deep in the pockets of my heavy parka, I trudged along on a deserted country road in the bleak depths of a New

Hampshire winter. It was January 1969, and I was about to turn twenty-four. I smoked my way through my second pack of Marlboros of the day, lost in thought as I contemplated how awful my life had become. I weighed three hundred pounds, I was in a marriage that had been a pitched battle for nearly three years, and I hated my job. I had no idea what I wanted to do with my life or whether I wanted to keep living at all. As my boots crunched along the hard-packed snow, my mind chewed on question after question: What am I going to do? How do I get out? How can I find my life?

The questions came at a feverish pace, stoked by a confrontation that had shaken me. It had occurred in the first session of a counseling class at the University of New Hampshire. I had gone to the university the first day of classes to begin a literature class, but I had found it so boring I left early and went looking for the friend, Neil, I had carpooled with. I knew he was a counseling student, and I wanted to tell him where to find me after his class was over. At the time, my knowledge of counselors was primitive at best: I thought they were mostly former teachers who helped kids fill out college applications.

I caught his eye through the open door of the classroom, and he waved me in to join the class. I thought this was odd, but I went in. Even odder was the fact that the students were all sitting on the floor in seven or eight small circles of half a dozen people. Neil asked me to join his group, and the others welcomed me with smiles and nods. Then they continued what they were doing, and what they were doing absolutely mystified me. They were talking about their own personal feelings and life issues! This seemed outrageous to me. One person talked about strains in her marriage, another talked about fears of making a key life decision. Another broke down and sobbed, and no one tried to stop her or comfort her. In fact, they seemed to encourage her to cry! I could not imagine myself talking about these sorts of things with anyone, but to talk about them in public was unthinkable. I didn't stay outraged for long, though. What happened next pushed me past my anger.

Suddenly one of the men in the group, a tall and bespectacled fellow with a bushy mustache, turned to me and asked, "Why are you so fat? Why are you trying to kill yourself at such a young age?"

My world stopped. I simply couldn't compute an answer. Finally I stammered out a semicoherent stream of babble about glandular problems and how there was nothing I could do about it and how I'd come to terms with it and everything was just fine. I flashed a cheery smile and shrugged my shoulders. The man studied me with an expression that looked an awful lot like disgust. "That's it?" he asked. "That's all you've got to say on the subject?"

I felt a welling up of fury at him, but I capped it and kept it contained. I just shook my head. The group looked at me with what I hoped was compassion but what I secretly feared was actually pity. It was a truly life-changing moment, but, perhaps as you have done in such moments, I resisted the opportunity mightily.

On that lonely stretch of road, on that bitter winter afternoon, I had become obsessed with his questions. I stayed mad at him for well over a week, during which all my defenses flared up as I tried to execute the messenger who had brought me this unwelcome news. Who the hell was he to hassle me like that? Was his life going so well that he could go around needling other people? Damned impertinence!

After a virtually sleepless week, it slowly occurred to me that being mad at him wasn't helping me feel any better. I began to wonder about his questions rather than blame him for asking them. This changed my life but in a way that was most unexpected.

Back to that moment of truth. As I turned toward home in the darkening afternoon, I stepped on a patch of bare ice covered over with snow. My feet shot out from under me, and I crashed flat on my back on the hard road. The back of my head smacked the ice, stars exploded in my field of vision, and I felt a blast of pain flash through my body. Suddenly I was in another world—not quite unconscious but a long way from my normal self. I was aware that my body was lying on the road, but I had no desire to move and couldn't have if I'd wanted to.

Next, I closed my eyes and saw with absolute clarity an inner vision I had never witnessed before. I could see down through all the layers of my body, mind, and soul.

First, the mind level: I saw that my mind had constructed elaborate defenses to keep my body from feeling the pain of my grief and anger and fear. I used my intellect to keep my emotions under control. Most of my thoughts justified my positions and made others wrong. I realized that I saw the world purely through my own projections. Because I was so out of touch with myself, I saw everybody else that way, too. I realize I had no idea who I was or what the world could actually be like: I'd made it all up and mistaken it for real.

Now I shifted to the body level: I felt how tight my muscles were, from the clenched fist of my stomach to the heavy armor of my shoulders. I realized I kept my muscles tight to deaden the pain of all my feelings. I held them in a locked position to control myself and keep from exploding.

I noticed all these things dispassionately, just as I might notice what time it is. There was no despair or "Wow!" to any of this incredible vision; it's just the way things were.

I shifted to the feeling level: I discovered I was awash in feeling and always had been. I had always prided myself on having no feelings, but now I saw the truth. Just because I wasn't letting myself consciously experience my feelings didn't mean they weren't there. There were so many that I didn't have names for them. It was like looking through a bowl of minestrone and trying to name the ingredients. I saw, though, that each feeling, no matter what it was called, had its own energy configuration. Fear was a certain pattern of waves of energy flowing from my belly, while anger was a very different energy shape. Anger had a jagged edge to it and a hot, raw sensation. It was dancing under the tight muscles in my neck and shoulders. Sadness was a dull throb of pressure in my upper chest and throat.

As I looked down through the levels of myself, I came at last to a clear space. Now I would call it my soul or my essence, but at the time what I saw was a vast open space that was at the center of me. The center was everywhere else, too; the space extended outside myself. In other words, it permeated the world as well as me and everybody else. Compared to everything else in me and the world—feelings, muscles, ideas, trees—the space was infinitely larger. It was most of what everything was made of.

As I lay on the frozen ground, I settled into that vast, clear space. I discovered that all the pain disappeared from my body if I relaxed into the immensity of the space. The vision deepened: I now realized that every single problem I'd ever had came from resisting the power and glory of this space inside me. Because I did not know how to live immersed in its vastness, I had assembled a set of acts that worked in the world to allow me to get along. When those didn't work, I had a more insidious set of acts to fall back on.

I got a clear answer to my fellow student's question, "Why are you so fat?" The reason: I was trying to kill myself to replay my father's life. He died at thirty-two, a grossly obese heavy smoker in a strained marriage. I was copying his life in uncanny detail. In the absence of any conscious purpose to my own life, I was doing his all over again.

As I relaxed more into the infinite space inside me and all around me, I could feel that the space itself was alive and yet vastly still at the same time. Between the clear space and the elements that it contained—feelings, body mass, thoughts—was a zone of subtle activity that was not quite pure space, not quite actual stuff. As I shifted my inner vision to see it, I realized that it was actually three things happening at once. I saw them as vibrations or shimmering waves, each with its own purpose and signature. As I searched to appreciate them, I saw that they were love, creativity, and intention.

Just next to clear space was the subtlest vibration, which I recognized as love. It was almost pure space, with just the lightest of vibrations. I could feel how love was the first thing that manifested out of the immensity of pure space. It was also the entry point to my soul: by loving we could open effortlessly to pure space.

Creativity was next to love. It was simply endless experimentation without judgment or criticism. In a word: play. I understood that we are at play all the time, and so is everything in the universe. I didn't enjoy it or realize it or let it work for me very much, but I saw that it was always going on anyway.

Love and play were flowing spontaneously from the center of pure consciousness. Then, just before things came into form, was the third zone of vibration: intention. The zone of intention was flavored with my particular history. I could see how I corrupted pure intentions with my own unconscious intentions. I could see how my intention to express my love had been thwarted by my life wounds and the wall I'd built around them. Because of this, when I tried to express love, it had a flavor of anger and fear to it. I realized also that my creativity was not being expressed clearly; it was often flavored with bitterness and cynicism based on my history.

In this moment I knew who I really was. Of course, part of me was the acts and the tight muscles and the unexplored feelings. But none of those were the essential me, because each of those acts and each of those feelings could have been different, and I would still be who I really was. This idea was deeply soothing to me, and I believe it changed my life direction permanently.

But then, with a groan of returning pain, I began to leave the space and come to. I saw clearly the levels of my self assembling again. I felt my tight muscles and my stuffed-in feelings and the thoughts begin to seethe in my head again. I felt deep despair that I had to leave this place and stand up in the three-hundred-pound body of one who smoked cigarettes and hated his life.

I stood up and got myself reoriented in the world. The back of my head throbbed, and a knot was forming. I glanced at my watch and saw that the whole experience could not have taken more than a few minutes. The knot is still on the back of my head. Doctors tell me I suffered a subcutaneous hematoma and have pronounced it harmless.

Although I felt a sense of sadness that I was leaving the magic inner world behind, I knew in another sense that I would always carry it with me. Now there was the promise that my life could take on a direction and purpose. I wanted to know myself to the soul-core so that I could live in that magic world all the time while functioning happily in the outer world.

I took a deep breath and headed toward home.

Bringing the Awareness into Reality

The project of reinventing myself with the soul side out would take some doing, but fortunately I only had to do it one step at a time. I dedicated my life to uncovering who I really was so that I could express my creativity and love in the world in their purest forms.

First of all, the weight had to go. For a month I ate only things that I intuitively felt would feed my true self. It turned out to be two things that I almost never ate—fruits and vegetables. When I would think about eating, I would tune in and find out what food would "sing to my soul." My soul foods were blueberries, carrots, greens galore, string beans, and apples. I shed thirty pounds in a month. I started feeling a little shaky from so little protein, so I switched for a couple of months to light proteins such as white fish and omelets made mostly of egg whites. I continued losing a pound every day or so. Then I alternated between the protein and the fruit-and-vegetable diet for a while. Within six months I had lost seventy-five pounds, bringing me down to 225. Maybe I wasn't a fashion model yet, but I was on my way. The last twenty-five came off much more slowly, but within a year I was down to around 200, eventually getting down to 180 or so.

At the same time, I lost a ton of psychic baggage by immersing myself in the University of New Hampshire counseling program. The classes were mostly experiential (we were still in the halcyon glow of the sixties, and education had not yet rigidified again). Consequently, it was like being in intense therapy for two years. I got in touch with my feelings again and learned how to give other people room to feel theirs. An unexpected surprise happened, partly due to opening up to my feelings again. My eyesight started changing for the better, and I soon was able to let go of my glasses and pass my driving test without them for the first time. My ability to see energy fields began to return, and I discovered how to put the skill to work in my counseling practice.

Dissolving the marriage was the most painful part of those years. My wife did not rise willingly to the creative possibilities of being single. In fact, our parting was the most bitter, awful experience I have ever had in my life. Even though the actual divorce happened fairly quickly, the fallout from it took longer than our relatively brief marriage. I wanted to move on so badly that I agreed to practically all her demands. She was from a moneyed family and had considerably more access to quality legal help than I did. Even though the divorce was financially devastating to me for many years, I eventually recovered. Emotionally, however, it took longer to build my reserves. It was a long time before I risked any kind of significant relationship again.

What got me through the pain was a deep inner knowledge of where I was going. I wasn't getting away from being a fat tobacco addict in a horrible marriage; I was going toward a life of soul awareness and creative fulfillment. Creativity also rescued me. One day I was talking to an inspired professor named Dwight Webb about my writing aspirations. I was telling him that I was having a hard time letting go of my desire to be a writer. I loved counseling psychology, but I'd always known somehow I'd be a writer. He made a simple suggestion. Why not write about counseling? Why not put all my feelings and inner experiences in the form of poems and articles for the profession?

It was an obviously great idea, but for some reason I'd never considered it. I was so inspired by it that I wrote a sheaf of poems about the counseling process. Many of these were published in counseling journals (and became my first publications in my new profession). The poems caught the eye of a professor at Stanford, helping me get a fellowship to that fine institution for my doctorate. I am eternally grateful to Dwight for his suggestion and have had the opportunity to thank him privately and publicly on many occasions.

I was on my way, with a literal smack on the head as my inspiration and guiding vision.

I told you about my first contacts with the living wisdom of conscious living—an easy one as a child and a second one the hard way on the icy road. Now I want to roll the clock forward to 1974, five years after my world-changing smack on the head in New England. This next episode will demonstrate how to get a lesson by feather rather than hammer.

In autumn of that year, with my new Ph.D. hanging on the wall, I was just days away from teaching my first classes as a graduate school professor at the University of Colorado. There was just one problem, though: I was convinced I didn't really know anything of ultimate value.

As I walked alone one pristine morning near my cabin in Green Mountain Falls, I was mulling over this deeply troubling issue. In spite of being trained at a prestigious institution famous in my field, even though I knew the research literature backward and forward, I felt utterly unequal to the task that lay ahead of me. The intensive years of work at Stanford had given me excellent clinical skills and had made a rigorous researcher out of me. But they had also separated me from my essence. Data-oriented research was the most highly valued endeavor. Personal experience was considered a source of distortion, not something to draw on for wisdom. Even though I was a master of a dozen powerful techniques, from biofeedback to hypnosis to empathic listening, I did not feel able to teach a single thing that resonated in my own soul. By spending those years in the research culture, I had wandered away from the contact with the living source of wisdom that had brought me there in the first place.

As I walked in the woods that morning, I felt a sense of panic building: Where should I go for the answers now? After all, I had studied with the best and wisest. I had read most of the key books in the field. Still, I did not have the thread that held it all together. What to do?

Suddenly an amazing idea leaped into my mind. Instead of reaching for answers, I could simply pose the questions—to the universe and to myself—and listen for an answer. Rather than straining at the leash of my consciousness, looking outside for the answer, I could stand still and listen. So that's what I did.

I asked these questions: Are we doing some single thing wrong that creates all our troubles? What can we do instead to create a life of happiness and productive service?

I stood beneath a tree and awaited an answer.

I didn't have long to wait. Seconds later, a cascading rush of energy streamed through my body, as if a torrent of passion had been released in me. The feeling was intense and electric yet completely benign. It was at the opposite end of the spectrum from scary; to surrender to it felt like the ultimate safety. I let go into it and reveled in it for minutes on end. I lost track of time during the experience, so I can only guess that it lasted a half hour or more. When the peak of the energy had subsided, I knew the answers to my questions. More important, I had reconnected with my inner source again. Possibly because I had asked specific questions, I received very specific answers. A life path began to open up for me.

Here is the awareness the torrent of energy left behind in its wake: we are doing one thing wrong that is at the root of our problems. We are failing to honor and love our authentic experience and failing to notice the authentic experience of others. When we are scared or sad, we try to distance ourselves from the experience rather than feel it, resonate with it, love it. We do not feel what we feel, and we do not tell the truth of our feelings to others. We live in a trance of denial in which we put our personality agendas ahead of connection with ourselves or union with others. These agendas of our personas—adopted in childhood for survival and recognition—are preventing us from resting at home in the vast space of our essence, which is something we could feel in our bodies and see in our minds.

I felt my essence again—who I truly was—as I stood there under the trees. Beneath all my feelings was the vast space of my pure consciousness. Beyond all my thoughts was the backdrop of consciousness—steady, clear, and radiant with serenity—and all of it was mine for the seeing. By resisting my experience all my life, I had trained myself to focus on illusion instead of reality. In that moment I let go of illusion and slipped into harmony with what is.

In that moment I woke up from the trance I'd slipped into in graduate school. Twice before—as a little boy and at twenty-four—I had experienced a deep contact with the source, and each time I'd gone back to sleep again. This third time must have been the charm, because I have never since lost touch with it. As I write now I can feel the imprint of that moment in my body.

That experience changed everything about my life. I realized that there was nothing to fear or hide inside myself. I began feeling the truth of my feelings and speaking the truth of them. The week before my experience, my girlfriend had asked me to say how I felt about her going to visit a former boyfriend on an upcoming trip. I told her it didn't matter, that it was "fine." Now I realized that I was covering my true feelings with my "cool California guy" persona. The old therapy saying was true: *fine* was a four-letter word for denial. In reality, I felt scared that she wouldn't like me as much and mad that she still wanted to see him. I felt hurt and confused; we'd been having a wonderful time, and now she was going away. After my experience under the trees, I told her all these feelings, and to my great surprise she seemed appreciative and relieved to hear them. She returned from the trip having completed things she needed to complete with the other man. She became much more present in our relationship.

The experience under the trees profoundly changed my therapy practice, too. Up until that day I would listen to a client's issue, then devise some solution that he or she would try out with more or less success. The solutions were all based on techniques that had been proven to work by the scientific literature. Suddenly now I could see the feelings that were running beneath the surface of the client's communication. I delved into those feelings directly, acknowledging them rather than looking the other way, and as my clients confronted the emotional depths of themselves unflinchingly, they moved very quickly toward resolving their problems. I found that people could devise much more ingenious solutions to their problems than I could, if they were given the room to go down through all their feelings to make contact with their essence.

Bringing My Life Path into the World

After that moment under the trees in Colorado, I felt secure entering the academic world. As my early books were published and my career took off, I felt that I had reached professional nirvana. I had everything I'd ever wanted.

In addition to teaching my graduate classes, I saw half a dozen therapy patients a week. I did this to keep from getting rusty, to have fresh data for theory building, and (truth be told) to supplement my modest salary. And for a while, all was well.

As I grew more experienced, I began to lose enchantment with the therapy model. It was so dreadfully inefficient. It seemed to me we were going about things backward. Rather than putting signs on the road that said Slow Down, Bump Ahead, we were training thousands of people to repair broken axles. Leaving behind a therapy model, I began to embrace a learning model, one that emphasized conscious living instead of remediation.

In the therapy model, you focus on the past, hoping that by shifting your perceptions it will lose its grip on you and free up more creative energy in the present. Sometimes it works this way; often it doesn't. The downside of therapy is that people often remain not only focused on the past but enthralled by it. Dependency on the therapist also becomes a problem.

In the learning model, you put yourself in the future and design conscious goals for your life. These goals, if you are committed to them, begin to pull you toward them. Along the way, old patterns may emerge similar to those addressed in the therapy model. The context is different, though; now you are engaged in a forward-looking journey of conscious living rather than a past-focused process of remediation. I found the learning model much more powerful. After all, have you ever seen a horse pushing a wagon along a country road?

I began to teach the learning model in addition to the therapy model, and the students loved it. They were delighted to learn the basic principles of conscious living that, when practiced, make much of therapy unnecessary. I would compare it to a medical school curriculum that introduced preventive medicine as well as remedial procedures.

I taught them the basic skills of living and loving:

- How to locate their feelings and name them correctly
- How to communicate clearly about their inner experiences
- How to make and keep agreements
- How to discover a life purpose and choose conscious goals
- How to love and accept ourselves as the foundation for learning to love others

In the seventies, I developed my career goal: to distill the essence of what people really needed to know about the art of living and bring it out in the form of books and seminars. It wasn't important whether the skills came from psychology, spirituality, or just common sense. The only thing that mattered was that they worked in the real world—in places like relationships, jobs, and health. The first seminar I conceived was called "The Art of Living," in homage to the ancient Greek philosopher of common sense, Epictetus. Six people showed up for the first session. Word spread, however, and thirty people enrolled next time, with nearly three hundred signing up on the third time around. The trend looked good.

After a while I started offering the course in a different format on the cable television network operated by the university. The first time the course ran on cable, one fan letter arrived. The message, though cryptic and scrawled in pencil, gave me heart. It said, "I'm not enrolled in your class, but I saw it flipping past the channels. What is this? It looks like you are talking about what it takes to have a happy life. Why isn't there more shows like this on TV? Thank you."

My sentiments exactly. When I replied to the letter, I thanked the author on behalf of Epictetus and Heraclitus as well as myself.

PART I

Finding Joy

Infinite Journey of the Questing Spirit

CHAPTER 1

Conscious Living

To make the most of our gift of life, you and I must answer two great questions in our short time on earth.

One question is: how do I live at peace with myself?

The second is: how do I live in harmony with people around me?

To answer these questions, we must find out who we are at our core. We must find out how to recognize the core selves of others. We must *learn how to learn,* about the most difficult thing of all—the ever-shifting needs and feelings of ourselves and people all around us. Thousands of years ago, the Greek philosopher Heraclitus compared it to dancing on running water, and it hasn't gotten any easier.

This book is a manual on how to accomplish the two main tasks of conscious living. It will show you a precise technology for producing inner peace and harmonious relationships. There are only a few main lessons you will need to learn and several conscious shifts you will need to practice every day. Once learned, these shifts are made as easily as looking up from the book you're reading and noticing the space that fills the room you're in. The shifts have been carefully researched in the laboratory of real life and passed down through the generations. You and I need to know these things—they are the required curriculum of life—and we need to know them now. The turbulence of our times demands that we find a firm place to stand so that we may reach for our highest potential.

Big questions like these cannot be answered in our minds; only whole-body answers will satisfy. It's of no value just to *know* how to live in peace inside ourselves or in our relationships. Unless we actually *feel* a core sense of well-being, unless we *feel* a flow of loving connection with our mates, intellectual debate on these questions is not only hollow, it is a pattern of defensiveness born of despair. We only argue about big questions when we can't feel the answers to them in our bodies.

The questions are urgent and always have been. If we do not find peace within ourselves, nothing we accomplish will feel satisfying. If we do not live in harmony with other people, we miss out on the very essence of life, which is feeling the glow of love as it is given and received with open hand and open heart. Conscious living begins for each of us when we commit to full engagement with these immense tasks.

I believe that all of us are seeking the same thing in life. Whether we know it or not, we are all on a journey. We have been going on pilgrimages, to therapy, to church, and to meditation retreats for thousands of years, seeking a richer flow of happiness and love. Conscious living is not just a philosophy; it is a living, organic source of wisdom you can feel in your body, understand in your mind, and apply to every moment of your life.

Conscious living is about how life actually works. It is not a set of beliefs or a faith. Think of it as you would think of the Colorado River, a direct expression of the laws of nature. You don't have to believe in the river or its creation, the Grand Canyon—it requires no faith—and you can experience it intimately by following the path created originally by a simple stream. If you come to the journey of conscious living with sincerity and an open heart, you will eventually assemble a set of practices you can use to embrace every moment of your life.

Conscious living gives you a somatic technology—one you can feel in your body—for moving through the most important challenges of living.

Conscious living focuses on the present, not the past or the future. It shows you how to open the flow of organic good feeling inside yourself and the flow of genuine love with others.

Conscious living is the art of full commitment to knowledge, balanced by full willingness to stand in wonder at the irreconcilable or unfathomable. Where the theologian might look for an explanation for the suffering of the innocent—karma, sin, reincarnation—the student of conscious living looks for a real-world way to relieve the suffering and stands open to wonder at the inability to resolve the paradox.

Conscious living shows you how to move through pain—whether it's pain of body, mind, or spirit—to make your home in a clear space of freedom. It shows you how you create unnecessary pain for yourself and reveals the preventive measures to avoid creating pain in the future.

Conscious living shows you how to redesign your life when you feel stuck, how to seize the opportunity that lies in the midst of difficulty.

It shows you how to channel your energies into what will truly fulfill you.

It teaches you how to embrace relationships that inspire your full capacity for intimacy and creativity.

It shows you how to live lightly on the earth and how to engage in social action that yields positive results.

It shows you how to bring forth your true potential and ultimately the great potential in all of us: how to give and receive love so that the full flowering of your essence and the essence of those around you is encouraged.

The Infinite Quest

I believe that conscious living represents us at our best. When we humans are at our best, we celebrate the questing spirit in ourselves. We seek, we wonder, we invent, we make mistakes and learn from them; the quest goes on. When the questing spirit lives and breathes in us, we are safe to be around. We inspire creativity by our very presence. We are good times waiting to happen.

For me, my journey of conscious living, which has taken me around the world over thirty times, began with a trip from one end of my grandmother's parlor to the other in a sleepy backwater town in the Deep South where I grew up.

My grandparents were still working on their bacon, eggs, and grits as I, a four-year-old, climbed down from my chair and solemnly bid them farewell. I told them I had to go to work, and they nodded gravely to acknowledge the pressing nature of my duties.

I mounted my new tricycle, just received the day before for my birthday. This rainy day I was given special permission to ride it inside the house, providing I obeyed certain traffic laws.

I pedaled carefully across the carpet to the other end of my grandmother's parlor, where I had set up a large cardboard box with a door and window cut out of it. I braked to a halt in the spot

I'd designated as my parking place. I stepped through the door into my office, resting my haunches on an orange crate. My grandfather and I constructed my "shingle," drawn in red crayon, which I now placed outside my office.

The sign said:

NOW OPEN
"PROBLEMS"

My life work was under way.

I made it very clear to my family that I would not give advice on medical issues; I considered physical problems not to be worthy of my attention. Any old doctor could fix those. I explained that I was a special kind of doctor. They were welcome to come to me with problems of how to feel better inside and how to get along better with each other. Since my vocabulary was limited, it was hard to get the idea across to them. Also, this was in a time and a part of the world where psychology and psychiatry were virtually unknown, certainly to me. But I had a deep inner knowing of what I was interested in. My province was the borderland between heart and mind and soul.

Business was slower than I expected. In fact, I don't recall any member of my family ever seeking my advice. They were a stubborn bunch who were more accustomed to dispensing wisdom than receiving it. For that matter, they were much more inclined to dispense wisdom than to practice any of it on themselves!

However, I can understand their lack of enthusiasm to use my services. It's probably not easy for the average senior citizen to accept advice on conscious living from a person in short pants, especially one who conducts his practice in a cardboard box and commutes to work on a tricycle. Call it the confidence factor.

Even though my practice got off to a modest beginning, I was confident that someday my time would come.

The Journey Makes Us Fully Human

At its simplest, conscious living is the art of feeling your feelings, speaking authentically, knowing your life purpose, and carrying out effective actions that contribute to your own well-being and the well-being of others. The moment we commit ourselves to living consciously, we embark on a journey of wonder through the real world, on a sacred path of infinite practicality. I believe that committing to the journey makes us fully human. I believe also that wholehearted participation in the journey is our very best way of returning thanks for the gift of life. Life comes to us freely; we wake up one day, and we're in it. Conscious living is the art of expressing gratitude for the gift of life by learning and loving as much as we can until the moment we're not here. Conscious loving is the art of learning and loving in our relationships—our relationship with ourselves and others—so that we eventually feel a continuous flow of love inside and out.

The lessons of conscious living are learned in the wide-open spaces of genuine curiosity, yet the open spaces have a path through them. The path of conscious living is paved with stepping-stones of wonder. Your wonder comes alive the moment you shift from conviction to curiosity. The wondering sojourner reaps a singular reward given only to those who keep their curiosity alive: pure, raw, unfiltered experience. One moment the raw experience may be blissful, the next moment unbearably painful or unfathomably confusing, but it is always genuine and direct and all yours.

The path of *unconscious* living is deeply grooved with well-worn ruts. Roles provide structure to the unconscious life, routines provide structure to the unconscious day, rules provide the safety of not having to invent anew. There is no doubt whatsoever about the popularity and pull of unconscious living. And for good reason. There is a certain kind of security in the path of unconscious living. It is the safety of being on a crowded bus and the surety that comes from being driven along the train track guided by rules and regulations. However, this kind of security comes with many costs. We may gain brief moments of security or self-righteous satisfaction by following the crowd to priest or guru for the answers to the big questions. However, those moments mount up quickly to become a life of comfortable numbness or sputtering indignation, ending with a snore or a fizzle.

When we are confronted with the big questions or the irreconcilable paradoxes or the unbearable griefs of life, we come face-to-face with the central choice of conscious living: whether to open ourselves in wonder to what needs to be learned or felt or resolved, or to contract into opinion, belief, and justification. Conscious living gives us a choice, presented anew in every moment. Every utterance out of our mouths serves one of two intentions: discovery or justification. Conscious living is a centuries-old art form of keeping our wonder alive in every moment, of holding the forces of stultification at bay so that the spark of consciousness can celebrate and create and play.

The journey of conscious living is a path of constant choosing. When you choose to step out of role and routine—when you find the courage to improvise and innovate so that you and others around you feel more vital and connected—this is conscious living. Conscious living is an improvisational journey of benign eternal vigilance, since we all have to be on the lookout for unconscious programming from our upbringing, our tribe, our genetic history. As the Taoist teacher of conscious living, Seng T'san, put it, "Our way is not difficult, save the picking and choosing." If we don't ask the big questions of life, if we don't find the courage to lift ourselves out of our backgrounds, we run our lives on default programming. That's unconscious living, and it has many seductions to beckon us, ranging from the couch comforts of the unexamined life to the riotous glee of a looting mob in full torrent.

Conscious Living Has a Rich Tradition

At the dawn of the Christian era, the quest for conscious living had already been going on for thousands of years. If you were in Greece and Rome twenty-five hundred years ago, you would find a flourishing school of philosophy that was asking the same questions we are asking today. These seekers were called the Stoics, named after the stoa, a colonnade in Athens where teachers lectured. At that same time, on the other side of the world, the Taoist philosophers of China were not only asking these questions, they were coming up with the same answers as their Greek and Roman counterparts a world away.

I have rested my hand on the stoa in Greece that gave the Stoics their name. I have hiked and biked up mountainous reaches in China and Tibet to find hermitages where Taoist monks taught and still teach today. I have sat with dozens of Eastern teachers and with hundreds of wise therapists of my own time and culture. I learned from these adventures that a living stream of wisdom has nurtured humanity for thousands of years. It is here for the asking, to guide us through the turbulent journey of changing times. Conscious living gives us a firm place to stand, but not a stand based on believing anything you can't see or having faith in something you can't experience right now. Conscious living has a greater gift to offer us than belief and faith. It gives us actual processes we can feel in our bodies.

When you can feel the radiant presence of the eternal universe right in the middle of a sore muscle or an aching heart, you don't need faith or belief. You have a living process you can rely on, one that works in good times and bad. You need faith only when you're not currently experiencing something good that you'd very much like to experience. You need belief only to keep you in touch with something you don't actually feel.

I can speak from experience because, in my own journey of conscious living, I've felt unbearable pain and unbearable bliss. I can tell you that I have felt the presence of the divine with equal intensity in very different situations—in meditation and prayer, in lovemaking, and in the dental chair while having teeth drilled with no anesthetic. The processes of conscious living—the very same ones we'll explore in this book—gave me that ability, and they can do the same for all of us. If you can embrace the divine while deep in meditation or while making love with your beloved, you are greatly blessed. But if you can embrace the divine in the middle of a root canal or a relationship squabble, you may be breaking new ground.

In this book we will focus on what works. I have discovered that what worked for the Stoics and the Taoists twenty-five hundred years ago still works brilliantly today. I was heartened to discover that the essence of what I had learned from thirty years as a therapist and teacher of therapists is the same wisdom contained in the self-change psychology of the ancients. The same deep river of wisdom has been running through humanity for thousands of years, reviving us any time we want to feel its flow and guiding us to the oceanic reaches of the world past the horizon of our normal comprehension.

The Holy Real

Although this book is a practical manual for living, it is also a book about the divine. In this book you and I will celebrate a special form of divinity: the holy real. On my own journey of conscious living I discovered a radical surprise: every aspect of reality is sacred. If we go deeply into what is real, we will find all the transcendence our souls crave. Things traditionally considered holy—angels, ghosts, visions of heaven, the presence of God—are all magnificent things to those who perceive them. Yet not everyone perceives them. Each is arguable, so much so that real people have been killed arguing over them.

Instead, we will enter a very different kind of sacred space, the cathedral of the real. In this holy place we can actually feel the soul in the body and the body in the soul. When we go deeply into the real—our needs, our relationships, our anger, our sexuality, our dreams and desires—we discover that the living, breathing vastness of pure consciousness is right there in the midst of all of them. Take any aspect of reality—even a harsh hot wind of anger in your chest—and take a few breaths into it. You'll find that within a few breaths the anger begins to dissolve in the light of your willing attention and the energy of your willing breath. In a moment your anger floats free in the open space of consciousness. A feeling of freedom appears and soon becomes the backdrop of everything we experience. If we focus on reality instead of fantasy, we can feel a spirituality that moves in our bodies.

I was an arch skeptic when I began my own quest many years ago. My skepticism melted in a surprising discovery: spirit is plain to see and easy to feel once we shift our focus in the proper direction. Behind each thought is the glowing radiance of the universe, between each breath the pure ground of being. There is a holy nothing at the center of everything, and it is *really something.*

This idea may sound cosmic—and it is—but it is also infinitely practical. Let me give you a specific example. A man sits across from me in my therapy office. His beloved wife is three months dead, and he is deeply depressed. The month before, he has attended a séance with a famous medium in an attempt to stay in touch with her. People in unresolved grief are food and diet to mediums, of course, and my client had experienced the usual "He told me things he couldn't possibly have known about her!" However, after the session the depression did not lift, and the medium said he needed to resolve many things with his wife, which would require a much lengthier and more expensive year-long series. He was undecided about this and sought my advice.

I withheld my opinion about the medium until later. Instead I offered him something very different.

"What's the one thing that you know of for sure that's real?" I asked.

"The grief, the loss, the sadness," he said, touching his chest.

"And to make it go away, you went to the séance to connect with your wife, so you wouldn't feel that horrible feeling."

He nodded.

"Then let me point out a real problem. For very understandable reasons, you don't want to feel all that grief. You even refer to it as 'the grief,' not 'my grief.' You want to distance from it. So, you're acting as if it doesn't deserve to be there. You go to a medium who says, 'You're right, it doesn't deserve to be there because you're wife's not really dead. She's still out there in a different form.'"

He nodded, beginning to get it.

"So, the medium is saying that your grief isn't holy, isn't sacred, deserves to be treated as 'the other.'"

His breathing deepened, and he began to sob.

"We're going to focus on the real—your grief and your loss and your confusion about what the purpose of your life is—and we're going to stay with it until you can accept that it's yours. Until, in fact, you can feel how sacred it actually is."

And that's what we did for an hour. I invited him to feel his grief as a raw experience, not filtered through the distancing mechanisms of beliefs about life after death. I invited him into the cathedral of the real, to make the grief in his chest a holy place. By focusing on the real feelings for minute after minute, an amazing transformation happened. At the end of the session he said, touching his chest gently, "This is where she lives now. She's with God, but God's in here."

He got to that realization with a searchlight of extraordinary power, a tool that is free and organic and available to all. It is the same searchlight that seekers of conscious living have been using for thousands of years. It's called wonder, and if we can learn to use it with sincere intent, it can take us everywhere we need to go. If you keep your wonder alive, you are on the path of conscious living. When your wonder dies—when you quit asking the big questions, when you settle into the roles and rules and routines (and, admittedly, the comforts) of a life of justification rather than exploration—something precious dies.

In hundreds of therapy sessions, I've invited my clients to bring in childhood photographs of themselves at different ages. Inevitably, one photo shows the time when wonder is no longer visible on the face. What happened? I ask. What killed your wonder? Who killed it? And how did you plug the hole it was ripped from?

As a child, I never resonated with religion; it seemed too concerned with hierarchy and rules and magical beliefs like heaven, reincarnation, original sin. It seemed too little concerned with the actual processes of living. I would watch family members come out of church and resume the same argument they had been grinding away on when they went in the front door an hour earlier. They had just hit the pause button for an hour to meet a social obligation. I was looking for something different: I needed a religion that stopped arguments. Later, I set about inventing my own religion—one I could feel in my body—and I then found that people like me had been doing the same thing for a long, long time. There was a rich tradition of people who were allergic to notions like belief and faith and angels and other things not observable to everyone in the room.

What Is the Journey All About?

When I got on my trike that day I did not know (at least consciously) that human beings have been on the journey of conscious living for at least a hundred generations. I believe the journey of conscious living is essential; the only choice is when we take it. I also believe that our lives are richly blessed to the extent that we consciously choose to take it. When I committed myself heart and soul to the journey, the blessings really began to pour forth upon my life.

Once I had committed myself to the path, I discovered an unexpected form of magic. A field of grace seems to form around us when we commit ourselves to something that satisfies our souls. Invisible pathways open up through the universe. We meet people who are on a similar path, and we are given forms of assistance that seem like magic. All these things happened as I opened myself to discovering who I was and what my true purpose in life was.

What had happened already—discovering my path to conscious living—was beyond my wildest dreams. But the best was yet to come.

CHAPTER 2

A Reliable Path

Make the best of what is in our power,
and take the rest as it naturally happens.

EPICTETUS

In my third decade as a therapist, I was working with a fearful patient who had left an abusive marriage years before but who was still recovering from the wounds of it. Like most experienced therapists, I do my best to engage both my heart and my mind when working with someone. My heart is trying to hold the person in an embrace of acceptance, while my mind is busily trying to find out what the person needs to learn, what principle needs to be mastered in order for the person to move to a deeper sense of well-being.

In this situation, it became clear that her problem revolved around the issue of control. Although she had left her husband because he had tried to control every moment of her life, she had taken over the job herself. She was trying to control her fear, partly through denying it and partly through holding her breath and her muscles tightly against it. Instead of accepting it, feeling it, and speaking the truth of it, she sought to hide it. These acts of control were making matters worse, like having one foot on the brakes of a car and the other on the accelerator. It makes for a jerky ride and eventually will burn out the equipment. I pointed out the problem to her, using the image of the brakes and the accelerator to get my point across. She visibly lightened up when she got the message. It was as if the cells of her body, which had been poised in a state of tension, suddenly relaxed.

I went further to tell her that fear cannot be controlled. Since it is already there, it is too late to change it. Better to flow with it—to let it be—and put your energy into figuring out what you need to do. Feelings are like rainstorms, I said, because they have a beginning, a middle, and an end. This odd notion—that the best way to get rid of an unpleasant situation is to quit trying to change it and let it be—took her by surprise and made an instant difference in her whole demeanor. She sat bolt upright out of the slump she'd been in.

"You mean that everything that's already happened is outside our control?" There was genuine awe in her voice, a tone of "Why haven't I thought of this before?"

I nodded. "That's right. You can't change the past. Plus, the things that haven't happened yet—the future—are also outside our control. You can plan for them and do things to influence them, but ultimately you have to let go of control and take the future as it comes."

Her jaw dropped. She said, "It feels like every ounce of my energy has gone into wanting my marriage to have turned out differently.

I've been so tied up in being mad because it didn't fit my expectations, I haven't had any energy to create what I want now."

I felt myself holding my breath at the eloquence of her words. She had just summed up the whole enterprise of therapy in a few short sentences. We keep ourselves so tied up in regretting the past and fearing the future that we don't have any energy left to figure out who we are and what we want to create right now. In the next two chapters, you'll see that this piece of wisdom is so important I call it the first lesson of conscious living. She had been out of kilter with the first lesson: instead of getting into harmony with reality—the marriage is over, and I feel sad about that—she had been fighting both those realities to keep them from being so. But so they were.

As she embraced reality as it actually was, her head sank toward her chest and tears began to flow.

Rather than talking her out of her feelings or telling her everything was going to be all right, I invited her to put the same principle to work with her sadness and anger. Let go of trying to control it, I said. Instead, be with it and breathe with it and flow with it until it stops organically. In other words, take the brakes off and feel what's real. She tried this out, and over the next few minutes she transformed before my eyes from a timid victim haunted by the past to a vibrant and forward-looking sojourner.

We said our good-byes, and she left my office. She was my last patient of the day, and after making some notes I sat back to enjoy the glow I felt. These are the magic moments of my profession. I wish I could say each session goes this way, but I have learned to be happy if one out of a dozen end with this kind of crescendo. I reflected on the wisdom that had been the pivotal point of the session. How much of my own life experience had it taken to learn this principle! How much of my own energy had I frittered away trying to control the uncontrollable!

My thoughts roamed further. Where had such a principle come from? Millions of people use the famous Serenity Prayer every day: God grant me the serenity to accept the things I cannot change, the courage to change those I can change, and the wisdom to know the difference. The prayer is based on the same notion, but I wondered, who came up with this idea? Then a small miracle happened.

My eyes lighted on a book across the room, one of several hundred on my bookshelf. It was Epictetus' *Enchiridion,* a slim book sometimes translated as *The Handbook* or *The Art of Living.* The book was written two thousand years ago in a time of frantic change much like our own. Epictetus was born a slave but because of his brilliance became one of the great teachers of his time. Then, when the first wave of Christian fundamentalism swept through Rome, he and most of his fellow philosophers were run out of town and banished to the hinterlands.

I took the little book off the shelf, wondering if Epictetus had anything to say about control. I flipped it open to the first page and read his first line: *The secret of happiness is knowing that there are some things you can control and some things you cannot.* I felt Epictetus wink at me across the centuries. There, in its most essential form, was the exact technology of conscious living I'd been using in my therapy session.

Ultimately, the journey of conscious living and loving is about making such moments possible. For us to share the infinite spaces of the core self with one another—this is life at its best, the thing for which we are best suited. The poet Rilke said that it was the task "for which all else is but preparation." To do that, however, we need to be whole within ourselves. Otherwise, our loving and living is an attempt to complete some missing part of ourselves.

We are designed to be one-selved organisms. When all of the multitudes we contain within us are embraced in the fullness and oneness of our core selves, we are happy. We can work, we can love, we can invent and celebrate, all in the large and loving unity of our core selves. When we're operating as one-selved organisms, we can connect with the one-self of our friends and family.

The task is never easy, though, because of a simple but profound problem: by the time we walk into elementary school, most of us are two-faced and two-selved—divided in mind, separated from our feelings, at war with our own bodies. We divide our selves in two for the very best of reasons: survival. To enable our true selves to survive in the often-perilous world of our young lives, we put on a false face for the world. Whether this face is a smiley face or a sad face does not much matter; the only issue is whether we can put our selves back together again later.

Conscious living is the art and science of putting our selves back together again.

Three Sources of Wisdom

Imagine yourself a hundred generations ago, hiking up a rocky path in Greece to ask a question of the oracle at Delphi. You would have endured harrowing ordeals to get there, and even more hardships would be required of you before you got to consult the sage. But over the entrance the real gift of your visit is written plainly for you to see. The sign says: Know Yourself. The metaphor here is powerful: if you want to tap into magic—to talk heart-to-heart with the divine—you need to know who you are. If you don't, no magic will save you. In fact, without a sincere inquiry into who you are, magic can destroy you or take you far astray.

I've spent over half my life watching magic unfold as people asked themselves, "Who am I?" As soon as we begin a heartfelt journey of wonder about our feelings, our needs, and the forces that drive us, we are rewarded with unimaginable riches of the spirit. But the journey must be taken with wonder, not with justification. I notice that many people sabotage their attempts at learning by approaching the subject from an intent to justify their position—making themselves either right or wrong for where they are and where they have been. If I ask myself "Who am I?" from a genuine place of wonder, I will get totally different answers than if I ask that question from an intent to defend or justify. I urge you to acknowledge and drop the powerful need to justify any aspect of yourself. I have learned the hard way that there is truly no need to do so. Much of my life was spent beating my head against the universe because I was asking the right questions from the wrong motive—the need to be right or to prove someone wrong. As I moved from justification to wonder, I found all the answers I needed seemingly in my cells and in the breeze around me.

I believe that we are heir to an organic philosophy of conscious living that can be understood in our minds and felt in our bodies. It is a gift we receive as we take ownership of a human body, a set of operating instructions that comes from the factory. You are welcome to call it whatever you like—Higher Power, Soul, Spirit. All I ask is your willingness to tap into it, whatever you call it, so that you can claim ownership of this source of wisdom and feel your organic connection with the many seekers of truth who have gone before you. Often, the stream of wisdom goes untapped in us, usually because the turbulence of life around us—family strife, emotional problems, poverty—puts our physical survival at stake. It is not easy to hear the chuckle of a flowing stream when your baby is crying or your rent is due. But it is always there, waiting for us to pause long enough to appreciate it.

In answering the question "What do we most need to know?" I will draw on three sources that not only have tapped into that eternal stream of wisdom but also have put it to great practical use. I will begin with the source I know most intimately.

The community of therapists and healers over the past hundred years has generated a comprehensive technology of change. As taught in most schools, though, psychology and psychiatry lack a spiritual base. These fields were developed partly in reaction to the authoritarian and dogmatic religious framework of the nineteenth century and so became extremely secular to set themselves clearly apart. In doing so, though, psychology and psychiatry failed to acknowledge the deep yearning for spiritual connection that lives deep inside us. The approach of conscious living is not in reaction to anything, and so it can openly embrace our secular selves and our spiritual selves. I learned most of what I deeply know about divinity by going through major changes in my life, assisted by the wisdom of the tools I will describe. Even though they are immensely practical, they are also deeply spiritual without calling themselves so.

The genuinely useful tools of therapy—those that have stood the test of time—are remarkably similar to two streams of wisdom that come from thousands of years ago.

One historical stream of teachings on conscious living comes from the Stoics of Greece and Rome. These remarkable teachers developed a powerful philosophy of self-change. The Stoics lived in a time when a philosopher was a combination of therapist and inspirational teacher whose province was the conscious encounter with daily life. Religion existed in that time, too, but it served a different purpose. Religion was concerned with appeals and offerings to various gods ordained by the state. It really had nothing to do with leading a moral or effective life. Only later, when the rational sanity of Stoicism had been combined with the magical heart of the new religion of Christianity, would religion become the mixture of mystery and morality that it is today.

The Stoic point of view is badly misunderstood today. Because of mistranslation and other factors, *stoic* has come to mean a steely posture of detachment and denial. Someone who can endure pain without flinching is often described as stoic. But if you attend carefully to what the Stoics were really saying, you will find little about denial. In fact, you will often find the exact opposite. The Stoic ideal was simple: live in harmony with the way things are. Let yourself resonate with your feelings and honor the feelings of others, then act from the open space beyond all your feelings. The original Stoics tell us: let go of your beliefs and expectations of how things must be. Ground yourself thoroughly in reality, then select carefully what you would like to change about the others, the world, or yourself. In order to change things, you must first embrace them as they are.

If you were going to pick one Stoic to read, I highly recommend the recent version of Epictetus' *The Art of Living,* carefully crafted by Sharon Lebell. She does a masterful job of bringing the essence of Epictetus into translucent modern prose. I also recommend *The Meditations of Marcus Aurelius,* although there's no translation of this work that has anything like the luminosity of Lebell's Epictetus.

Another profound stream of teachings on conscious living flows from the Taoists of ancient China. It has always been wondrous to me that both the Stoics and the Taoists began expressing many of the same ideas at the same time, about twenty-five hundred years ago. It's as if a dawning of wisdom shined on the Mideast and on China at the same time, bringing forth a light that still radiates today. The *Tao Te Ching,* in its many translations, remains one of my favorite books.

In the seventies I made many trips to the Stillpoint Foundation, a Taoist center in Colorado, to sit with its founder, the late Gia-Fu

Feng. Gia-Fu translated two Taoist classics, the *Tao Te Ching* and the *Inner Chapters of Chuang-Tzu.* We usually sat cross-legged on his floor, surrounded by Chinese, English, and German translations, sipping tea together. Most of our time was spent poring over individual passages, commenting on how various translators had handled the concepts. Gia-Fu also loved to sit in a bathtub for hours, hot water up to his chin. Many of our visits took place with him in the tub, while I sat on the floor of the bathroom, trying to keep the books dry when he would flail his arms excitedly over some idea.

Sometimes Gia-Fu would get inspired, and nuggets of his own Taoist wisdom would come out of his mouth. One example still makes me chuckle. I had found a passage (in the twenty-first chapter of his translation of the *Tao Te Ching*) where I thought he had put his own spin on the verse, taking it pretty far from its original meaning. He was interested in Gestalt therapy, and I was gently needling him about giving the passage too much of a Gestalt flavor. He reflected for a moment then said, with admirable nondefensiveness, "Yes, I think I took too many liberties there." Then he sighed happily and sank a little deeper into the warm water. "Ahhhh," he said, "always best to receive criticism while already sitting in hot water."

I feel privileged for the opportunity to immerse myself in the living presence of the Tao rather than simply to learn what I know through scholarly contact.

The great beauty of conscious living, whether its wisdom is drawn from Taoism, Stoicism, or your neighbor next door, is that it puts a set of practical tools in your hands. All of the great teachings of conscious living contain not only concepts but also "shifts" and "moves." A shift is an idea that is so useful and clearly expressed that you can feel it in your body. A move is a concept so applicable that it shows you how to dance and grapple with the real problems that come at you every day. Shifts and moves are so practical you can use them to move through difficult times in your life or to heighten your happiness during the expansive times. Conscious living has given us a wealth of shifts and moves, and I'll do my best to describe the best of them as our journey together proceeds.

CHAPTER 3

Five Required Lessons of the Journey

In this chapter we explore five key lessons of conscious living. These ideas have changed my life, and I have watched them change thousands of others. As you master the lessons, you are being taught by life itself. The ideas all put you in direct relationship with the universe so that you get your teachings about living straight from the wholesaler. The five cardinal lessons of conscious living are all ways of taking charge of your life and finding your place in the universe. Taking charge can sound like a willful move requiring a lot of effort, but in this case it's not. Here, you take charge of your life by resonating in harmony with the way the universe works.

Resonate with these ideas in your cells, and you can put away your icons and gurus. You were probably never comfortable with them anyway. When I fully understood the core ideas of conscious living, it was as if the universe itself said, Smile, friend, you just got your soul back.

If you look back over your life, you will find that you keep getting certain lessons repeated over and over until you learn them. The same thing is true for other seekers and has been for thousands of years. Certain lessons are so profound, and so tough to master, that we can get stuck on one and spend an entire lifetime butting our heads against it. As I have worked with people in my career, and as I have studied the great teachers of conscious living of the past few thousand years, I realize that we all need to learn five foundation lessons of living. If we learn them, life works. If we don't, it doesn't. These are the required lessons of conscious living. Everybody gets the same challenging lessons, usually every day, and we define our lives by whether we resist learning them or embrace the challenge with passion and willingness. Unfortunately, many people wait until the death rattle is gurgling in their throats before they wake up, with an ultimate gulp, to the same lesson that was first presented to them on the front end of life.

Here's an example of the five required lessons of conscious living:

Feel all your feelings deeply. Throughout our time on earth, human beings have had moments like the one I am about to describe. I've had them, and perhaps you have, too. These are the moments when the cardinal lessons of conscious living are brought to bear on an urgent problem in our lives. I'll describe the lessons as thoroughly as I can later in this chapter; for now, though, watch and listen as they come to life in a most practical way.

You are alone one evening, feeling sad about the recent loss of a close relationship. You have been left, and this has never happened to you before. You have the urge to distract yourself from the painful feelings by eating some chocolate or turning on the television. But you have made a commitment to living more consciously, so you don't distract yourself. A new path opens to you because of this commitment.

You face your feelings straight on, putting your attention on the sensations of sadness in your chest and throat. You rest your attention there for a few seconds, then you feel a shift. You are still aware of the sadness, but a clear spacious feeling opens beyond and through the sadness. Now the spacious feeling expands, perhaps comparable in size to a large playground, while the sadness is a lone child playing in solitude on a swing set. From this spacious new view, you realize you have sadness, but it doesn't have you. You feel a deep sense of relief flow through you. You realize that while the sadness has come in response to some event and will probably go as you come to terms with it, this spacious clear feeling is your permanent home. It is who you really are.

You have just learned the first cardinal lesson of conscious living: feel all your feelings deeply, and feel your way through them to the vast soul space in which all feelings are embraced. By facing all your feelings and resonating with them deeply, they lose their grip on you so that you can act from a clear space informed by your feelings but not run by them.

Seek your true self. Next, you realize the loss was inevitable. Perhaps you pushed too hard for the relationship to work, overlooking the cues that it just wasn't right for either of you. As you accept the sadness and the loss, an insight comes to you. You realize that the relationship was founded on one of your personas, a social mask you adopted for survival early in life. In this case, the persona is Caretaker, although it could have been one of the many we all wear. You formed the relationship so you could take care of the person, and that was not what the other person wanted. So it ended, as all things must end that are founded on a false front. You wonder, who am I if not a caretaker? Who is the real me underneath all my masks? A feeling of the authentic you begins to form inside you, and you make a commitment to form your next relationship out of this new and growing sense of your true self.

This is the second cardinal lesson of conscious living: make all your life a quest for the discovery of your authentic self. If you put the highest priority on your inner life, your outer life will thrive because it is rooted in a sustainable and self-nourishing base.

Let go of the uncontrollable. Out of this new awareness your mind is suddenly jumping with possibilities. You get a taste of serenity with the following moves: you let go of trying to fix the old relationship and feel a sense of acceptance of it, just as it is. The past already happened—it is completely out of your control. So you let it go. You accept your sadness and all your feelings, realizing you really never had any control over them anyway. Your mind and body slip into a sense of ease, no longer trying to control the uncontrollable. You wonder, what exactly can I change or control about this situation? Well, you can pick up the phone . . . so you do. You call the person who left you and say: I've finally come to accept it all, just as it is. Thank you for everything. You put down the phone and realize the evening is far from over. You have control over whether you go out or stay home. You go to a bookstore and spend the evening browsing.

By letting go of trying to control the uncontrollable—by accepting reality as it is—and focusing on those things you *can* control, you learn the third lesson of conscious living. It begins to work its magic on you.

We are all made of the same thing. While browsing in the religion and spirituality section, you give birth to a radical new idea inside yourself. You realize that you have always gone outside yourself for your spiritual and religious teachings. You are not wrong for doing this, but you open yourself up to a new possibility. You see that your old approach has been based on a false notion—that you are somehow spiritually lacking and that you must make up for this lack by consuming the predigested spirituality of others. Now you let go of this fallacy and feel an internal shift: you are a spiritual being at the core. You don't have to do anything different to become spiritual; you already are as spiritual as you're going to get, and so is everyone else. All you have to do is let go of trying to be what you aren't, anyway! The spiritual core of you has been there all the while, just waiting for you to accept it and own it as yours. The feeling of your own organic spirituality flows through you, and you feel reborn.

This is the fourth lesson of conscious living: that we are made of the same stuff as everything else in the universe. Everything is alive and equal—the shortest path to the true spirituality in the universe and in ourselves is to go inward toward our cores, not outward toward other people's experience.

Life is fullest when we're most true to ourselves. As you walk home, exhilarated by the new feelings flowing in you, you pause to look up at the stars. You realize you could be a star in your own universe. You wonder, am I courageous enough to tap the deep wellspring of my creativity and express it boldly in the world? As you walk along, you ask yourself, what would I most like to create, both for my own nourishment and for my singular contribution to the world? Three things pop immediately to mind: you want to write poems, you want to play the cello again after many years' absence, and you want to walk the Lake District of England. By the time you are home, you have made plans to take a poetry class, play your cello in a nearby nursing home, and, for information and inspiration, watch a friend's video of her trip to the Lake District.

This is the fifth lesson at work: that life reaches its full flowering when we bring forth our creative desires and the treasures with which we have been blessed and act on them in the world.

Life is trying to teach us these five lessons in every moment of our lives. If we learn them, life becomes joyful and fulfilling. If we do not, we come away from the banquet of life hungry and dissatisfied.

These five lessons hold the fundamental truths about life that everyone needs to know. Both the Stoics and the Taoists taught them, and they figure in thousands of therapy conversations every day. These truths are so powerful that therapists could probably make a successful practice using them as their sole therapeutic technique.

Let's go into each of the lessons more deeply, beginning with the principle that is the very foundation of conscious living.

The First Lesson of Conscious Living: Feel All Your Feelings Deeply

Always and in every moment, embrace what is real inside yourself and focus on what is real outside yourself. Embrace all your feelings—pleasant, unpleasant, and neutral—and realize that all of them occur in the larger space of your essence, who you truly are. Your feelings have a beginning, a middle, and an end, and none is more important than another. Your essence is who you truly are, beneath all your feelings and if all your life experiences had been different. Through your essence you are connected to the same space that everything in the universe rests in. When you let your feelings be free to come and go—when you stop resisting them or clinging to them—you rest in your permanent home, a clear and unwavering perspective from which to take actions that benefit yourself and others.

The principle can be said many ways. A poet might say, identify with the sky rather than the passing clouds that obscure it. A body surfer might say, deal with life as you would the ocean. Feel a part of it—enjoy your immersion in it. When waves come, rise with them and bob over them, or use their energy to ride toward the shore of your chosen goals. Don't turn your back to them or shut your eyes to them. Not only are the waves real, they are an expression of the divine. To flow with them is to touch divinity. To ignore them is, at best, to miss out on life and, at worst, to be buffeted by them and perhaps destroyed.

No matter what words we use, the first lesson invites us to open our hearts to reality as it actually is, to celebrate it without putting any spin on it. When we make our home in the space that holds everything, we are less likely to be captured by fluctuations of thought and emotion. We have a firm place to stand, in the space that at first seems nowhere but eventually can be seen everywhere.

At first you might not think of space as a firm place to stand. Indeed, when I first discovered it myself, I went through a period when I was confused about who I was. Suddenly I could see and feel my personality, but I wasn't really attached to it. When I relaxed into space—that which holds all personalities—I realized that my personality was like a playsuit I could don for interacting in the world with other people dressed in the playsuits of their personalities. None of the playsuits were any better or worse than any of the others, and none of them were really who we were. Our personalities were simply based on agreement. For survival purposes, usually early in life, we agreed that we needed to be "dependent" or "domineering" or "cute," and the agreements had usually been made unconsciously before we walked into kindergarten. When I identified with my personality—when I thought that was all I was—I had to make it right and defend it against others. If I shifted my identity to the space I felt inside me, suddenly I was free. I could own a personality without it owning me.

The same thing turned out to be true with my feelings and thoughts. When I identified with a certain feeling—for me it was usually anger—I was trapped within it because I either made it right or made it wrong. If I made it right, I was trapped inside the false notion that someone else had caused my anger. If I made it wrong, I hid it and tried to shame it into submission. Neither position worked very well. I could flip-flop back and forth all day making my feelings either wrong or right, and they would still be there when I went to bed. The only freedom came from shifting my identity to the space that contained all my feelings.

All my thoughts, all my opinions, all my precious points of view—those, too, were traps when I identified with them. If I made any point of view right or wrong, I glued it into place and decreased my freedom. I had spent so much of my life having opinions and defending my point of view: now I realized that they were all exactly the same, just places where I glued my foot to the floor and limited my ability to dance. I put myself on an opinion diet, in which I avoided forming new opinions and quit defending the ones I had. My wife liked this diet a lot; she thought the new slimmer version of my previously fat head was much more becoming.

As human beings, we suffer from a grand illusion. We think that safety comes from contracting around our opinions, making them right and then defending them. The problem with doing life this way is that we then must clump together with other people who share the same opinions, seeking the larger safety of the herd. When you put a bunch of people together who share the same opinions, you might think that all would be happy and harmonious. But it actually works the other way around. Soon the whole tribe will unite under an authoritarian leader and troop off to do battle with another group that has different opinions. Even when there's no "other" to fight against, the group will break up into factional squabbles, form secret societies that only one gender can join, and other such troublesome ways of whiling away the time between wars.

The only real safety is to be found in the space that holds all opinions. In this space, I came to realize that all my opinions and everyone else's were exactly the same. They were all ways of viewing the world from one position. We were all bent over, hunkered and huddled in our positions, peeking out backward from between our legs, thinking we were seeing the world the way it was. In this position we were not only limiting our perception, we were ripe for the kicking.

And kick us life does; it must do so until we can expand to see things as they actually are. However, of course, it's us doing the kicking. All of us are connected to space, whether we contract away from it or expand to embrace the world from the safe expanses of it. It never goes anywhere. Most of the difficulties we experience in life are our own way of teaching ourselves the first lesson: take all of life as it comes. Feel it, breathe with it, let it go. There is a space inside from which all things are as they are, free to come into existence and pass away. That space is what I choose to celebrate, and as I honor its serene vastness it grows even more immense within and around me.

The first lesson invites us to resonate with life and to feel our way through to the larger space of our whole selves. Think of yourself for a moment as a beautiful acoustic guitar. Life is always playing on our strings, and sometimes none too gently. If we try to arrange it so life doesn't get to us—so our strings are never plucked—we don't get to hear the music. If we let our strings go slack through disuse or lack of care, we never get to know what we could sound like. If we keep ourselves in tune, we can hear all the overtones and vibrations of ourselves and our neighboring strings. It is the space within the guitar that makes the sound what it is. If we become sensitive, we can hear the silent space at the heart and soul of our instrument, the very source from which all the sound emerges.

The First Lesson Is Not About Detachment

A shallow understanding of the first lesson has led some people to accuse the Stoics and the Taoists of detachment. But the first lesson does not teach a state of detachment at all; it is a celebration of yourself and life from a viewpoint of the whole. By opening your heart to all of life—but clinging to none of it—you are participating in life fully. You are not freezing any part of life and saying "This is it!"

The first lesson teaches us that reality itself is holy. The anger you may feel emerges from the wholeness of yourself and contains the wholeness within it. If you allow your attention to rest on it nonjudgmentally, you will discover the happy surprise that I have seen on the faces of thousands of therapy clients: your anger will dissolve into the whole again. Quantum physicists as well as mystics tell us that everything contains the wholeness. The divine nature of the universe is there for the looking and listening, even in the aspects of life that seem most mundane.

The first lesson creates peace inside yourself, and it also works its magic in your relationships. Once you make your home in the vast space of essence, you start seeing other people's essence much more easily. You don't get caught up in other people's emotions and their projections onto you, because you can see who they truly are in their essence. Genuine relationship—meeting other people essence to essence—finally becomes possible.

I certainly wish I'd known this wisdom during some of the hard times in my life. There was a long period of my life when I felt estranged from my true self. Because I had no true home within me, I thought my personality was who I actually was. I thought I was nothing more than a striver and a pleaser and a doer. Because I had no open space in which to hold my feelings, I was run by my feelings, either denying them or being carried away by them or justifying them. It never occurred to me to be with them or simply to acknowledge them. Because I had not found the "being" of my human being-ness, I took all the transitory comings and goings far too seriously.

The Power of Essence

There is a great deal of power in finding the space of pure consciousness within ourselves. Once you feel it you can never have any more doubts about the divine nature of the universe and your connection to it. The space you feel in your body and mind feels seamlessly connected to the space-at-large in the cosmos. The space feels organically divine, as the drinking of water feels organically thirst quenching compared to seeing the formula for water written on a chalkboard. The Zen writer D. T. Suzuki called it "the lightning-and-thunder discovery that the universe and oneself are not remote and apart, but an intimate, palpitating whole."

In the twentieth century, the Native American visionary Black Elk spoke his version of the principle this way: "The first peace, which is the most important, is that which comes in the souls of people when they realize their relationship, their oneness, with the universe and all its powers, and when they realize at the center of the universe dwells the Great Spirit, and that the center is really everywhere. It is within each one of us."

Coming from a very different perspective—quantum mechanics—the physicist David Bohm said essentially the same thing. He suggested a primal state of oneness, which he called the implicate order, in which everything is enfolded and from which everything emerges. Everything in the universe unfolds and becomes itself out of this space of wholeness. Each element of the universe contains within it the wholeness from which it came. We are enfolded in the wholeness of the cosmos, and it is enfolded in us.

Part of the beauty of the first lesson is how simply you can prove this magnificent idea. A ten-second experiment will remove any shadow of doubt. Take anything unarguable in your experience right now—perhaps a heaviness in your shoulders or a recurring thought in your mind or an anxious feeling in your stomach. Rest your attention nonjudgmentally on this bit of reality, and let it rest there until you feel a shift. If you stay with this experiment for a few seconds, you will likely feel the following sequence of sensations. Perhaps you are focusing on tiredness in your shoulders. At first you will be aware of the sensations of tiredness as something solid. It may feel like a block or a band of tension. As your attention continues to focus on the sensations, they will seem to shift into a shimmering sense of movement. Now you don't feel anything solid; instead there is a tingling or buzzing or throbbing in the same place as the solid sensation used to be. If you stay with these new sensations, you will experience the true reward of the experiment a few seconds later. Suddenly a spaciousness will appear where you were feeling a block not long before. How does this occur?

It occurs because what is looking—your consciousness—is also what you are looking for. Consciousness itself is at the bottom of everything, and everything about us emerges from it. Therefore, when you consciously use your consciousness to study anything, it quickly finds itself. It has to, because it is the backdrop and forefront of everything.

The Answer to the Question: Who Am I?

The first lesson speaks to the heart of who we are in the universe. It says that we are equal parts of the whole, and to pretend that we are special cases is not only a fantasy but a potentially disastrous one. As Thaddeus Golas, the author of *The Lazy Man's Guide to Enlightenment*, says, "We are all equal beings, and the universe is our relations with each other." We must be wary not to embrace any belief that takes us out of oneness with the universe. The moment we do so we render our force field dense and impermeable. The moment we begin believing we are fallen angels or risen apes or reincarnated lamas, we cease resonating with the wholeness of all. Then adversity begins and will not cease until we again embrace the oneness.

This idea has tremendous practical value. When we resonate with the whole, we open ourselves to an intimate connection with the matrix of support that our universe is. There is no doubt that the universe is supporting us constantly. As an example, think back to the beginning of your life. You may have been unplanned or unwanted at conception, and you may have been subject to many different beams of negative energy while your mother gestated you, but all the while you were drawing support from an entire matrix that surrounded you. You were drawing nurturance out of another person's very bloodstream, and even though it may have been contaminated with nicotine or alcohol or fearsome thoughts, it still was enough to allow you to survive.

Today, as we move through the world, you and I are supported by a vast matrix of people and things who are there for us. The person who bolted your steering wheel into place, the citizen of Macao who made the sweatpants I am now wearing, the geniuses who thought up and built this amazing machine on which my fingers tap out these words—indeed, those who taught me how to write and you to read—all of them are part of the matrix of support in which we live. I do not often pause to acknowledge the matrix—to express thanks for all it has done for me—but when I do I feel better for it. When I have acted on that gratitude, by such actions as writing a note of thanks to my graduate school professors or the minister of the church of my youth—I feel more connected to myself and the world around me.

The first lesson shows us how to establish contact with our essence and resonate in harmony with the wholeness of the universe. When we're ignorant of who we really are, and when we're out of touch with the rest of life, we cannot act. We can only react. Nothing genuinely creative can come out of us. But as we embrace the first lesson, suddenly everything changes. Knowing who we are at the core, feeling in harmony with our surroundings—this is our starting place. From there we can move into the world of action. Then our actions are flowing from a space of wholeness. The second lesson of conscious living now becomes relevant.

The Second Lesson of Conscious Living: Seek Your True Self

The second lesson says, *Get your priorities straight. Focus first on who you are, then let your actions flow from this place of deep self-knowledge.* Your inner life must be fed and nurtured as much as your physical body. Do not focus on appearances and external achievements while letting your inner life languish.

Many of us live backward and upside down. We put our attention on appearances. We fail to base our outer lives on a living, breathing, and continuous inquiry into who we are at the core. Without a central hub, the wheel of our lives cannot turn effectively.

This lesson has tremendous practical value. It has made my life infinitely easier and more successful. Before I discovered the second lesson, I handled resistance completely differently. When I would encounter resistance out in the world, I would either give up or try to beat my way through it. I took the resistance as real, as something that actually was occurring externally. I don't want to suggest that you were hallucinating those seven red lights you encountered on the way to work this morning. They were no doubt real. But they might have been green had you been less in a hurry. In the old days, I spent so much time cursing the traffic lights that I never got around to asking the key question: what is it about me that is causing me to encounter all this resistance?

Let me give an example of how this lesson can shape a life. In the seventies I found myself split in half on a particular issue. I was drawn with my heart and soul to applied psychology and spirituality. I wanted to focus my writings on practices that any person could put immediately to use in everyday life. Bolder than that, I thought we should rename the whole field of psychology, calling it conscious living. When people entered a psychology class, they should walk out the door an hour or a semester later knowing how to live their lives more effectively. I felt strongly that the truly useful parts of psychology were really about helping people live by design instead of default. Here I was, an academic psychologist—first at Stanford, then at University of Colorado—when I suddenly found myself waking up to a most painful realization: most of academic psychology is worthless and, far worse, wastes the energy of many bright people.

I had a negative epiphany one day when a brilliant new student from the Middle East showed up to fulfill his dream of studying psychology in America. He told me that his professor had just put him to work studying the behavior of a certain species of ants when light was shined on them. "I am very disappointed," he said. "I cannot tell my father, who has sacrificed so much to send me here, that I am watching ants. I had a different idea of what psychology was about."

My teeth ground silently. "So did I," I said.

However, I was teaching in the graduate school of a large university, where to get promoted one had to focus on publishing articles in the research journals of the field. I published some of these articles in the first few years of my career, but I did it grudgingly and halfheartedly. It felt like a waste of time to me, especially when compared to the excitement I felt when I was doing what I really wanted to do.

Even at the conservative research institution of Stanford, I had argued with my professors that we should take our powerful concepts out of the ivory tower and "into the streets" where people could use them. I felt that we had something so valuable that we should make every effort to put it into people's hands. This was in the days before self-help books were popular, so I did not have any examples to point to. I knew in my heart, though, that people were interested, if we could only find a way to get the information to them.

The day that changed everything—the day I put the second lesson to work—started with an unpleasant experience. My first book was to be published any day, and I was eagerly awaiting its arrival. It was a book of relaxation and focusing activities for teachers to use in the classroom, to help children feel more alert and relaxed. Finally the day came, and I opened a package to find not only the sparkling new book but also a piece of wonderful news. It had been selected by a teachers' book club as their book-of-the-month offering, which meant it would go out right away to thousands of practicing teachers. This outcome was beyond my wildest dreams.

Nearly hopping with excitement, I showed it to a colleague who was standing at the mailboxes sorting his mail. As I burbled enthusiastically about the book club, he picked the book up and peered at it disdainfully. Without opening it, he handed it back and said, "I suppose it must be fun to write things like that, but what's the point?" For the same expenditure of energy, he said, I could have done some real psychology (by this he meant an experimental study with statistics in a journal with small typeface). Turning away with a rueful shake of the head, he said he wished he had time to "write just for fun."

I felt angry at his put-down, but beneath the anger was a deep sadness and a fear. The sadness was about not being appreciated for my contribution, and the fear was that maybe I was on the wrong track. (I later found out that jealousy may have also played a role in this conversation. He had written a classroom workbook for teachers a few years before that had sold only five hundred copies before going out of print.)

I sat down at home that evening and felt the pain of my colleague's withering contempt. My mind alternated between blame and shame. One moment I would think about how wrong he was, but the next moment a burst of thoughts would emerge about how it was all my problem. As my feelings deepened, my mind cavorted through leaps of overgeneralization. Soon I was the lone misunderstood genius doing battle against the forces of anal fundamentalism threatening my beloved field. Then a shift occurred: I suddenly realized that I would continue to feel this split as long as I wasn't clear about my purpose. If I were grounded thoroughly in my purpose—what I was really up to—I could communicate it effectively so that my colleagues at least knew the force behind my actions. If they didn't applaud my activities, they would at least respect them because they flowed from a coherent set of intentions.

And that's exactly how it turned out. As I sat in my house, I asked myself the following question: what is the purpose of my life? At first nothing came, but as I wondered about it, an answer began to form, much as a photographic image swims into focus in a darkroom. When it finally became clear, I felt a sense of peace and ease descend throughout my body. My purpose was this: to expand in love and creativity every day and to assist those who are interested to expand in their ability to be more loving and creative. From that moment on, I had in place the organizing foundation of my life and work.

The great value of knowing your purpose is that it gives you an instant checkpoint for evaluating any action. Is this serving my purpose, or is it not? My university work shifted dramatically. I quit trying to be something I wasn't. I was much more interested in the world of relationship and connection than I was in the world of statistical significance and confirmation. Most of my important learnings about my field had come from a moment of contact in which something crucial had happened. I had never read anything in a journal that was as useful as simply sitting with a therapy client for an hour.

As I became clear about my purpose, I began to articulate my values. I became a public spokesperson for an intimate, heart-centered form of research that did not use traditional statistics. Suddenly my colleagues seemed to change. They dropped their disdain, and first I got their grudging respect, then a measure of the real thing. To my great amazement, I even received the annual Outstanding Researcher award one year! It seemed miraculous to me at the time, but later I understood that this is one of the effects of knowing your purpose.

Respect from outside is a fine thing, but inner respect is crucial. It is difficult to respect ourselves if we do not know what we are doing and why we are doing it. If we do not come from a place of clarity of purpose, and the respect for ourselves that flows from it, none of our actions will be fruitful. This Stoic idea was adopted into the popular new religion of Christianity and is beautifully expressed in the book of James: "A double-minded man is unstable in all his ways."

There are many ways of finding out your purpose. I have found that the biggest barrier is that we think it is going to drop in on us from a mystical source outside ourselves. After helping a number of people discover their purpose, I have found the exact opposite to be true. The best way to reveal your purpose is to let it come from inside. To find it, ask yourself questions like:

What do I most love to do?
What could engage me so deeply I'd never want to retire?
What am I really about?
What would be a purpose so grand that it could express itself through everything I do, from shoveling snow to making love to sitting on a bus?

As you shift into deeper resonance with your purpose, your goals will also clarify. Clarity of purpose seems to call forth clarity of the specific ways it should be expressed.

The first and second lessons of conscious living teach us to embrace ourselves deeply and to open to a deep sense of connection with the universe and the inhabitants of it. Because you know yourself better, and because you feel connected to the whole, your evolution picks up speed. You now need a major navigational tool. It is the third lesson of conscious living. Epictetus urged us to use it, as did a dozen other philosophers and thousands of therapists. I have personally seen it make miracles occur in the lives of people the moment they grasp it.

The Third Lesson of Conscious Living: Let Go of the Uncontrollable

How do we cut through the morass of information that comes at us all day long? How do we make sense of all the thousand and one moments of thought, feeling, and action that make up our day? The human mind, if unchecked and unfocused, will leap back and forth between fantasy and reality, past and present, hundreds of times an hour. It will chew obsessively on some irrelevant idea that has no possibility of making you happier or more creative while completely overlooking an obvious possibility that has genuine value. The ancients recognized this problem and came up with strategies to deal with it. Epictetus, the Stoic, found the following principle so important that he opened his manual of conscious living with it:

The secret of happiness is knowing that there are some things you can control and some things you cannot.

This lesson by itself is a powerful tool for self-change. I have used it to revolutionize my own life and have shown many therapy patients how to use it to revolutionize theirs. I have mentioned elsewhere that I was an obese child, at one point over a hundred pounds overweight. I used the third lesson in my weight-loss program, accomplishing something few people do. I'm told that over 90 percent of people who lose a large amount of weight eventually gain most of it back. I'm not one of them. I lost a lot of weight and have kept it off for twenty-five years. The third lesson is part of the reason why.

Most people cannot muster the energy to change because they are consuming their energy focusing on the unchangeable. We might sit at home fretting about a troubled relationship, for example, while completely overlooking the simple step of picking up the phone to call the person. The same is true for weight loss. None of us can control our weight.

Imagine there are two files in our minds. Let's call the one "Things I Can Control" and the other "Things I Cannot Control." Weight definitely belongs in the file called "Things I Cannot Control."

If you think you can control your weight, go stand on the scales and decide to lose five pounds. You will notice that the scales do not move with your decision. (If you were able to make the scales go down five pounds by deciding it in your mind, contact me immediately for an exciting business venture.) The fact is, we have no control over our weight. Yet many people obsess about their weight constantly while it goes up and up and up. I have worked with clients who weigh themselves twenty to thirty times a day. Their obsession with the uncontrollable uses up all the energy that could be channeled into focusing on things within their control.

Two things that influence your weight are in your Things I Can Control file: what you eat and whether you exercise. If you accept the reality of what you weigh and cease obsessing about it, you then have energy to focus on what you put in your mouth and whether you exercise today.

Our lives begin to change only when we take full responsibility for the venture, and for this venture we need all our resources. This requires that we let go of focusing on things that are out of our control and bend our awesome energies toward those things we can control.

When I began looking at my weight problem from this perspective, a radical new possibility opened up. I quit worrying about my weight and put my attention purely on things that were within my control. I thought carefully about every bite of food I put in my mouth. I dropped thirty pounds in thirty days and felt better than I ever had in my life. I bought a cheap bike and took my first bike ride in years. Soon I was hooked on daily exercise. Within six months I had lost seventy-five pounds or so, with more coming off more slowly over the next six months. Twenty-five years later, I still have a body that gains weight very easily. But I continue to exercise every day and watch what I put in my mouth. These things are within my control; my weight isn't.

Most things are not within our control. Other people, whether they like us or not, their feelings—indeed, our own thoughts and feelings—are mainly outside our control. Those things obviously cannot be controlled, but there are other things not so obvious.

Even if there is something that is within your control, such as exercise or eating vegetables, don't bother to focus on it unless you have commitment and a plan. If you can't control it, and if you don't have commitment and a plan, you have only one healthy alternative: pure acceptance. By *pure* I mean unconditional, total, down-in-your-body acceptance in which you let go of any attempt to control it. There is great power in this move. Alcoholics who benefit from AA change their lives with this move. They stand in front of a group and they say, "Hello, my name is ______, and I'm an alcoholic." They admit they are powerless over alcohol. They call it the way it is by saying they can't handle it. Up until that day, they may have spent years trying to convince themselves, their family, and friends that they do not have a drinking problem. Letting go of defensiveness and accepting their alcoholism frees up energy for the key enterprise: not taking a drink this day. It works because of the third lesson. By accepting something you can't change or control, you can focus all your attention on something that you have total control over—whether or not you pick up the glass and pour liquor in your mouth.

The third lesson works with feelings, too.

If you are walking toward an elevator and you feel an old, familiar fear, the last thing you should do is try to control it. You couldn't, anyway, because if you could control it you probably wouldn't have chosen to feel it in the first place. Without question, fear is beyond our control. Herein lies the power and the prize. If you cannot control it, the only sane alternative is to relax into pure acceptance of it. Like a surfer encountering a big wave, you can ride it to a larger version of yourself. The essential step, however, is getting on the elevator. No matter how much you are accepting your feelings, it is the action step that counts. Getting on the elevator is made much easier if you accept your fear rather than resist it. The moment of acceptance puts you into harmony with yourself and acts as a springboard to useful action.

The unhealthy alternatives are so dismal as to make contemplating them painful. If you don't accept reality as it is, you are condemned to resist it. You sentence yourself to a moment or a lifetime of wishing you were not having the experience you are having while you are doing nothing to change it. This is indeed hell on earth. Even in hell, though, acceptance is only a breath away.

I first felt the full power of the third lesson in a time of dark depression. Once upon a time I was by myself in a mountain cabin, feeling lost and lonely. My girlfriend was away, visiting her other boyfriend, so I was feeling jealous as well as lonely. My old VW was rusting and battered, I had fewer than a hundred dollars in the bank, and it was freezing and miserable outside. Standing in my living room, staring at the fire, an idea came to me. I could accept all of it just as it was. Rather than wishing I felt some other way, rather than wanting my whole life to be different, I could let go of my control and accept it as it was. As I dropped my resistance, I felt a rush of energy course through me. What probably happened was that all the misery turned to light and energy, just with my turning my mental nozzle from "Resist" to "Accept." My inner feeling turned to pure ecstasy—wave after wave of it—and it lasted for three days! I would not have believed that such a thing was possible before experiencing it. Such is the power of the third lesson.

The Fourth Lesson of Conscious Living: We Are All Made of the Same Thing

At least five hundred years before the Christian era began, a remarkable notion surfaced in the Mediterranean and in the Far East. Later we would read it in the Bible as "The kingdom of heaven is within," but in an earlier form the idea was expressed by Epictetus like this: "You are a distinct portion of the essence of God, and contain part of God in yourself." Hundreds of years later, the prophet of Islam would say it like this: "Those who know themselves know God."

Wherever we stand and wherever we go, we carry the universe and its divine essence with us. This is a radical idea—from the Latin *radix,* meaning "root"—because it reorganizes our perception of ourselves at our very core.

The fourth lesson says: *When we go deeply enough into who we are and who others are, we will find our organic connection with divinity and theirs.* When our conditioning is cleared away, what remains at the core is the divine essence of the universe floating within us. Go inward to taste the divine, not outward toward the synthesized experience of others.

Suppose you have a pain in the neck. You can treat it as an interloper, an offender, a plot against you. Or you can treat it as something to learn from—indeed, a friend. Either way, you can take a pain reliever, but in the second instance you can learn something at the same time.

Let's say you take the learning path. You begin by wondering about the pain. What put it there? When did I first notice it? Was it when I first awoke? Or was it just after that unexpected phone call from my boss, telling me that I'd messed up once again?

Questions like these sound ridiculous to many people. I can tell you, from treating hundreds of people with chronic pain, that a particular type of person who thinks these questions are ridiculous is precisely a person with chronic pain! People who suffer from chronic pain will be the first to tell you that their pain has nothing whatsoever to do with them. They absolutely hate the idea that their pain could be caused by something they're doing. They particularly hate the idea that it could have anything to do with their failure to express their feelings in commonsense ways. They love the idea that their headaches are caused by cloudy weather, negative ions, yeast, biorhythms, bad genes, and several hundred other attributions I've collected from pain patients over the years. They love the idea that their pain can be cut out, rubbed out, numbed out, cracked out—any kind of "out." The cosmic paradox here, of course, is that this very way of thinking—"My pain is wrong and must be banished"—is exactly why they hurt in the first place.

But you decide not to think that way with your pain in the neck. You adopt a view, suggested by the fourth lesson of conscious living, that there might even be divinity in your neck pain. You could use something so mundane as your very path to the divine.

So you inquire into it. You play with it, turning your head this way and that. You discover an "A-ha!" It's connected to a pulling sensation between your right shoulder blade and your spine. Rather than stopping there with a "so what?" and a soda pop, you inquire further. You play with the connection between the pain in the neck—No! *my* neck!—and that little place near your shoulder blade. Suddenly a thought leaps into your mind. The pain started the night before, when you saw a news report about a tragedy that you felt helpless to do anything about. You realize that you felt angry about the harm done to innocents, a bomb falling on a school bus, but you didn't know what you could do about it so you forgot it. But your body didn't forget. It remembered all night long and woke up before you did to remind you today.

As you make this connection, you realize that your neck pain is fading. But you don't stop there. You continue to explore the sensations, and then you get the big payoff. You feel connected to those innocents on that bus. You open up to your heartfelt connection with the wounded innocents on that bus and the wounded innocence inside you. Your pain is their pain, and their pain is yours. You realize that there is no such thing as separation in this world or any other. You realize further that pain is caused by separation, trying to pretend that we're "different from" or "other than" something else.

Not only is your neck pain gone, but you have replaced it with your original cosmic connection to the world. We are all one and all divine. Even neck pain is an expression of the divine, if we know how to tap its spiritual potential.

I've treated chronic pain that way for two decades. I've got mileage on this idea, and it works. I've watched hundreds of people slowly eliminate headaches and back pain from their lives by using exactly the procedures I've just outlined. In a few memorable instances, it's happened so quickly it seemed like a virtual miracle unfolding before my eyes.

The idea of the fourth lesson was crucial to the Taoists as well as the Stoics. It is also a concept modern therapists use every day, whether they realize it or not. Therapists teach that the organic process of the human being can be trusted. If our clients are sad, for example, we invite them to feel the emotion deeply instead of talking them out of it. We invite them to go inward with their attention, toward the source of the feeling, rather than outward. This approach is based on the fourth lesson. It is saying, you can trust yourself, because ultimately you will encounter the divine if you take your attention far enough inward. Therefore you have nothing to fear along the way. We know, along with Black Elk, Epictetus, and Lao-tzu, that the far depths of ourselves are made of the same stuff that organizes the whole universe and that ultimately there is only the vast expanse of space inside and out.

Many people get stuck in a dilemma when they think of changing their lives. They wonder, is it better to choose goals and apply their will to creating what they want in life or to live goal free and open to the flow of the universe? The secret is to do both. To live a full life we must be open to the Mystery and live a purposeful life within its spacious context.

The Stoics and the Taoists would like us to leave the space alone, not to clutter it with beliefs about it. "Never lose a holy curiosity," said Albert Einstein, inviting us never to explain away the mysteries of existence. We come out of the ultimate Mystery, and into the Mystery we will go. While we are here, let's not seal off the Mystery but keep it alive, celebrating it each moment. Do not settle for easy answers for the Mystery. Enjoy the Mystery, dance with it, raise a toast to it, but do not pretend to know all the answers to it.

This notion runs counter to much of the fundamentalism that pervaded the ancient world and has resurfaced in our time. For fundamentalists, there are ready explanations about the Mystery. They know who made it up and who is supposed to represent the Mystery on earth. Wars have been fought over these issues, and millions of people have died because of differing explanations about the Mystery. For Stoics and Taoists, though, nothing that can be argued about is worth arguing about. They feel that it is best to appreciate the Mystery—drink the water instead of arguing about the chemical formula for it—and not get too attached to any particular theories about it.

Ultimately, say Stoics and Taoists alike, spiritual progress comes from confronting grand realities of life—such as death and misfortune—unflinchingly and free of fantasy. Looking at the facts and the calamities of life without illusion increases our ability to stay centered in essence and allows us to see the deeper wisdom in all nature's phenomena. Above all, the steady gaze at reality allows us to see what needs to be done—if anything—and what must be accepted as it is.

The Fifth Lesson of Conscious Living: Life Is Fullest When We're Most True to Ourselves

If you express what needs to be expressed within you, you will be happy and fulfilled. If you don't, you won't.

It's just that simple, but many of us spend our lives making it more complicated. We go to great lengths to tune out what needs to be expressed. We tune out through liquor, gossip, and drugs, or we stare hypnotized at the flickering television images.

Sometimes what we must express are secrets. We often seal off the shameful and painful moments of life. Cut off from the fresh air of consciousness, these concealed pockets of pain fester until they are brought to the light. I have seen miracles occur in the lives of hundreds of people after they shared a guilty secret. More dramatically, I have watched with awe as life-threatening diseases left people's bodies after bringing forth an age-old secret. Some years ago I was asked to do several sessions of therapy with a man who was bound for prison. His attorney was also a client of mine, and he asked me as a favor to work with the man to help prepare him for the shock of losing his freedom in his midforties. Although he had steadfastly proclaimed his innocence, a jury had convicted him of the crime. To my great surprise, the client confessed after two sessions that he had actually committed the crime. It was as if life itself was entering his body as he came out from behind the cloud of deception he had been living in for a year. He still went to prison, but it became a transformational experience for him. His prison sentence became a time of spiritual growth, during which he organized literacy programs for other inmates and carried out other acts of service.

Sometimes the secret is a withheld potential. "You are a poet," I said once to a midlife therapy patient after she had shared with me a heartfelt and beautifully written section of her journal. This offhand comment set her in motion writing poetry, something she had not done since junior high school. Over the next few months I watched in awe as torrents of poetry poured out of her. This new self-image changed her life. It was as if part of her had been asleep since adolescence, waiting to be breathed into life by the right circumstances. Now, as she came into full wakefulness, her confidence grew as a poet and a person. Next thing I knew, she had published several poems and performed a public reading. And this from a person who had once been so afraid of public contact that she wouldn't even hold a garage sale.

The fifth lesson teaches us that peace of mind comes only with full participation in life. This means being open to the full range of ourselves, from the quiet background throb of our hidden feelings to the cascading torrents of creativity waiting to be brought forth.

In Summary

Twenty thousand therapy sessions during the past thirty years have taught me something I now believe in my bones. We choose how gently we get our lessons by how open we are to learning. Life teaches us with a sledgehammer if we refuse to pay attention. It administers the same lesson with a feather tickle if we show a willingness to learn. The journey of conscious living might well be called a journey from requiring sledgehammer blows to allowing ourselves to be tickled into clarity. Learn the five required lessons, and you can retire your hard hat. Instead of getting bludgeoned to death, you can tickle yourself into infinity.

CHAPTER 4

The Inner Shifts and Outer Moves That Create a Conscious Life

Now let's find out how to apply the five lessons of conscious living to the everyday problems we all face. I have found that the principles are brought to life through shifts of consciousness and what I call "moves." The great value of conscious living is that it teaches us how to practice the principles with our whole bodies. Without these whole-body moves, there would be no value to the process; it would be an empty set of ideas.

As children we learn the concept of crossing a street safely, but it is the whole-body move of looking to the right and left that actually keeps us safe. I've spent much of my life helping people learn the moves that make a conscious life, and I have often despaired that we wait so late in life to learn them. In an ideal world, instead of teaching things like the names of state capitals in elementary school, we would teach the moves. I remember spending a week or two slavishly memorizing the state capitals, a body of wisdom I seldom draw upon. In fact, I've been waiting forty years for somebody to ask me the capital of Montana, poised to burst forth with "Helena!" So far, the information sits idly in long-term storage. Those same weeks could have been spent teaching me the following moves, and it would have given me skills I could use every day to make my life better. Indeed, knowing these skills would have saved me many waves of pain in my life.

The moves are as easy as shifting your eyes from looking at one thing to looking at another, yet they are as profound as the movement from caterpillar to butterfly. They require practice, but once learned they are like swimming or riding a bicycle. You cannot go back to not knowing how.

Here is a beautiful story from the Zen tradition that shows what I mean. A new student was talking to a Zen master about where to start Zen practice.

"Where should I enter Zen?" the student asked.

"Do you hear the murmuring of the stream behind us?" the master asked.

The student listened, then said yes.

"Enter there," the master said.

Once that shift has been made—from not hearing the stream to hearing the stream—we can never go back. From now on, it is simply a matter of practice, of learning to pay attention.

We create a conscious life by how we handle tiny and very specific moments. From thirty years of helping people, I have learned beyond a doubt that we are shaped more by choice than by our genes and our past history. These things certainly play a role, but what I have really seen is the awesome power of choice. I see that we are presented with the same choices over and over again, and our destinies are shaped more by those choices than by any other factor.

Our schools and particularly our churches do us a tremendous disservice by teaching us to focus on our beliefs. What they should be teaching us is how to make the choices that lead to a conscious life. Plenty of people are chock-full of beliefs about spirituality, but many of those same people make choices every day that pervert and prevent spirituality from becoming real in their lives.

The choices we will explore occur in four main areas: facing, accepting, choosing, and taking action. When I spell them out on a chalkboard, I often write it like this: F*A*C*T, with an asterisk or star between each component. I am hinting that each move contains within it the keys to our stardom.

Here's how it works.

The First Key Move: Facing

Everything begins with a choice to face something or to avoid facing it. Facing is the choice that saves the most lives. Failure to face something is the choice that destroys the most lives. If you are not happy and creative, look first at what you are not facing in your life. When our lives are not working, there is always at least one thing we're not facing. We may not be facing that we:

Hate our job
Have a drinking problem
Are in love with someone else
Need to take better care of our body

Or a thousand other things. At the bottom of our problems is always something we're afraid to face. We will often destroy our lives to avoid having to face it and, worse, take others—sometimes innocent children—down with us.

Whatever it is, imagine turning to face it squarely. This is the move. To keep it simple, look first in three places.

There may be a feeling you are not facing. You are not allowing yourself to feel something consciously. For example, you may feel guilty about something, and that feeling gnaws away at you until you acknowledge it consciously. You may be angry about something or scared or hurt. Feelings need to be faced. If not, the energy that it takes to keep looking away from them exacts a cost on your whole life. Feelings are the first place to look.

The second place to look is anyplace you are not facing the truth. The truths are usually straightforward and obvious. You may have done something you feel guilty about, and you haven't come clean to the relevant person. You may be angry at someone or hurt by something the person said, and you have not told the person directly. When we don't communicate the truth clearly, we don't feel good. Your inner self will keep reminding you, in the form of unbidden thoughts or unsettled body feelings, until you communicate what needs to be said.

The third place to look is agreements you are not keeping. There may be an agreement you have broken and haven't cleared up. Perhaps you told someone you would do something and you didn't follow through. Or you told someone you wouldn't do something and you did it anyway. These moments of slipped integrity register in our inner selves, and we are charged for them by unsettled feeling, if nothing else, until we handle the broken agreement.

The majority of unhappiness in life comes from these three places. Face these first, and you are going to move toward greater well-being. Make a practice of living in the following question: what do I most need to face right now in my life?

The Second Key Move: Accepting

The second key move is accepting. Facing is seeing reality; accepting is harmonizing with it. Once something has been faced, it must be welcomed into the wholeness of ourselves. If you face, for example, that you are sexually attracted to someone other than your partner, you have definitely made a crucial move. Many people do not face such things squarely, and by not facing reality they create a rattle inside themselves. But it can't stop there. In order to get the rattle out, you have to accept all of the feeling into all of yourself. There are depths to every feeling; usually the flickering tip of it is what is in our awareness when we first tune in to it. There may be deeper levels of it, which are where the real learning is. You may tune in deeply to your sexual feelings for someone other than your partner, for example, and find that it is not about sex at all. The sexual feelings on the surface are real, no doubt about it, but the deeper you go the more you find that it is really about a yearning for a certain kind of connection with your creative energy. This happened to me awhile back, so I can speak of it at first hand.

I felt some sexual attraction for another woman in 1995. Kathlyn and I fortunately have two agreements that made the process that unfolded much easier. One agreement is that we are committed to hearing the unvarnished truth from each other. Another is that we are committed to telling each other the truth as soon as we're aware of it. The initial attraction took place at a party, so I was able to tell Kathlyn about my feelings within seconds of feeling them. She felt angry and told me so but then appreciated me for leveling with her. I let myself feel the sexual attraction consciously rather than harboring it as a guilty secret. I told the other woman about the feelings, too, and the three of us spent a (stimulating) twenty minutes talking things over.

As I kept tuning in to my feelings, I became clear that I did not want to have actual physical sex with her. As I listened to my deeper self, I realized she was a metaphor for something I was losing touch with in myself. She was young and vital and free spirited; I felt I was losing those qualities in favor of becoming a prosperous citizen. As I opened up to accepting the sexual feelings, I also opened to accepting a part of myself that I really needed to look at. I was rolling into my fifties, and although I was reaping the harvest of twenty-five years of focused work, I was also losing touch with the impoverished but passionate young fellow who could get all his belongings into his VW bus. I kept having fantasies of driving off into the redwoods of northern California in a VW bus with the young woman in question, her shimmering blond hair blowing in the wind. We would live in the woods, far from fax machines and the $30,000-a-month overhead. We would grow organic vegetables, swim in mountain streams, make love with abandon.

Accepting these feelings consciously made me aware of many other things I needed to accept: the loss of youth, the inevitability of death, the need for a way to bring wildness back into my life. As I welcomed all this into myself—not without the screeching of my psychic brake pads on occasion—I felt connected with my essence again.

I realized I had drifted into the seductions of comfort and its traveling companions, rust and sluggishness. I was losing touch with my essence in favor of trying to be all things to all people. By reaching a certain level of success in the world, I had developed an entourage of dependents: staff members, family, publicists, and the like. Everyone seemed to want something from me, and they seemed to need it by yesterday. I had been overlooking a brushfire of unconscious resentment that had begun to smolder in me. Thank goodness for the sexual attraction to the magnificent young woman who caught my eye. By following the feelings to the core, I learned something about me that no actual physical encounter could have given me. In fact, a physical sexual relationship would have locked me in to a drama that probably would have obscured the real issues beneath the surface. My relationship with Kathlyn became much stronger after this experience, and the wild woman who inspired all this has become a treasured friend to both of us. In fact, she and her husband-to-be invited us to help officiate their wedding.

I don't think I could have reaped such a rich harvest of learning unless I accepted and told the truth about all of me—sexual feelings and all. By doing so I was flooded with awarenesses that enriched my life in unimaginable ways. I learned to live in this question: what most needs to be accepted and welcomed in to the wholeness of myself?

The Third Key Move: Choosing and Committing

There is a moment when you must decide something significant. Following the choice there is a moment of commitment. Do you put your heart and soul into your choice? When I was thirty-five, I fell in love with Kathlyn and invited her to move to Colorado to be with me. Then I faced a further choice: would I commit fully to the relationship or stand on one leg, my other foot out the back door? Making halfhearted commitments was an old script for me. I was beginning to wake up to the possibility that my unwillingness to commit was based on a deep fear of getting too close to another person. I realized the folly of my position just in time and brought both feet under me to stand firmly in the relationship. On one magical day, I looked Kathlyn in the eye and said, "I'm here. You can count on me. I make a commitment to you that's bigger than my pattern of running away."

It is only through commitment that choice becomes real. Almost two decades later, my relationship with Kathlyn is alive, precious, exhilarating. And none of it would have been possible without the choice and the commitment. That's why I say, if you do not feel good, look for where you have not made a choice. Next, look for where commitment is lacking. Beneath every life drama is a choice waiting to be made, and commitment will bring the choice into living reality.

Ninety-nine percent commitment is not possible. We are either committed 100 percent or not committed at all. I was amazed to discover this, because I had made a lifestyle out of tepid commitments that turned out to be noncommitments. I was just conning myself that I was partly committed. I had adapted to the pain of early rejection with the decision "Don't play." If I didn't play, I wouldn't have to face losing. And if I were forced to play, I could always play halfheartedly. If I lost, I could say it didn't matter, because I wasn't trying. It took me many years to realize that I wasn't even in the game if I was not committed. My body might have been out on the field, but my soul was on the bench. Soulless play is worse than no play at all.

The Fourth Key Move: Taking Action

Imagine standing on the diving board twenty feet above the water. To get there, you have faced your fears and chosen to climb the ladder. You are committed to the jump. None of this matters, though, until your feet leave the board, until you launch yourself into space. The action step is everything.

Until we take action, our potential lies in reserve. Without action, my friends could say at my memorial service, "He was an accepting guy, and, boy, could he face reality. He was terrific at choosing and committing. Unfortunately, he never did anything. However, we suspect he could have." I wouldn't want that kind of memorial service for me.

Better to throw ourselves into life. Buckminster Fuller once said that his success was due to a single factor: he was willing to make more mistakes than anyone else he knew. I feel blessed to have figured that out at an early age. I got out of a marriage that wasn't working in my midtwenties, even though my mother pointed out that "it was the first divorce in the history of our family." (To her credit, however, she pointed this out only a couple of hundred times!) Later, bless her heart, she confessed that her disapproval was based on envy. She secretly admired my tendency to go for the bold, to do things others might not try. Hearing this eased my mind and made me appreciate her, and myself, more.

In this moment, and a thousand others, I learned to ask myself: what action is the crucial next step?

The Freedom Is in This Moment

I feel grateful to have discovered the power of these four moves in my life. I have come to have great respect for their power and for the power of our resistance to them. I watch people in therapy go to great lengths to avoid facing something or to avoid a commitment or an action. I often wonder why we resist these moves so much. If only we could see that our limitations are largely made of nothing.

Take the past, for example. We think of it as something, but it is really nothing. Go looking for it, and you will never find it. We all think of ourselves as being shaped by the past, and many of us think we are limited by it. The truth is, you and I both have a past. It's been powerful and often painful and has shaped us in ways past knowing.

Having said that, I invite you to forget it. The past is, quite literally, irrelevant. It has power over us only if we give it the power each moment. You give it power by the moves you make in each moment. Each day you and I are offered the opportunity to recreate the past or to create a brand-new future. Take your mind off the past and the future, and focus instead on moments that are occurring constantly. If you do this, I guarantee you will not regret it.

No matter what has happened to you in the past—no matter where you've been or what you've done—you, like me, are creating your life this moment through your choices. You are choosing to read a book this moment instead of sticking your hand in a baseball glove. I'm not saying you are making the right choice; all I'm saying is that you are making a choice. I happen to like your choice, but now and then I also like to stick my hand in a baseball glove.

If you think you are your past, you give power over your choice to things outside your control. The past has already happened, and you cannot do anything about it. What is real is this moment, and you have ultimate choice when you're in it.

Our personalities are revealed by how we handle moments of choice. I was dining at a Moroccan restaurant awhile back with a group of people, some of whom were friends and some of whom I did not know well. As our meal was winding down, a belly dancer took the floor. During a certain part of her performance she invited members of the audience to join the dance. The choice contained many possibilities. We could have some wild fun and express ourselves in a new way while supporting the belly dancer in her act. At the same time, there was a high potential of making fools of ourselves.

Another fellow and I got up and danced.

I'm not saying we made the right choice or the best choice, but we defined ourselves by the choice we made. Other people at the table revealed their personalities through their choice. One person said, "No way, I can't dance," revealing an ingrained limitation. His mate said, "I won't unless he does," revealing her dependency on his leadership in the relationship (which she complains about frequently). Another person jokingly said it would be undignified (but, joke or not, it kept her from dancing). Another averted her eyes shyly from the whole scene.

The two of us who danced had a wonderful five minutes of energetic hilarity.

I once saw a short poem tacked on the wall of a monastery I was visiting:

There are fools who dance and fools who watch the dance.
If I must be a fool, let me be a dancing fool.

My friend and I revealed ourselves as dancing fools. The point is this: all of us define ourselves by our moments of choice. The question is whether you and I will make our choices based on who we have been in the past or who we want to create ourselves to be right now. I vote for creating ourselves based on a positive present and a future we choose consciously. That's what I am up to. As I study my life, and the lives of those with whom I work, I notice there are particular moments of choice that have incredible power over our destinies. We may think destiny is a big thing, but it is really created in tiny moments.

Each of us faces several specific moments of choice that determine whether or not we will have a happy and successful life. I cannot overemphasize the importance of these moments of choice. They may seem subtle or simple, but they have life-changing (and life-threatening) consequences. I've seen a wrong choice send a person into a downward spiral that has taken years to get out of.

Let's begin with a choice we encounter hundreds of times a day.

The Essence Shift: The Choice About Where We Place Our Attention

The first choice we face is where to place our attention. Will we focus on a small piece of our consciousness, or will we choose to focus on the essence?

I would like to consider this first shift from several angles, to dwell on it more than the others, because it is the heart and soul of what needs to happen to create a conscious life. Let me take you inside the shift by describing a personal experience.

I am walking down a city street, on automatic pilot. I am successfully crossing streets without mishap, and I am dodging the hurrying bodies rushing past me. Otherwise, I am oblivious. At the moment I notice my obliviousness, I realize I have been replaying the same conversation in my mind over and over, each time making a minor alteration in it. Trouble is, the conversation happened yesterday. There is no reason for me to be obsessing about it, except that I must have some leftover feelings from the conversation. Sure enough, as I tune in to my emotions, I realize I am irritated by some of the things that went on in the conversation. As I make the shift from being lost in my thoughts to being in touch with my body sensations, I feel my breathing deepen and my body relax.

Then I choose to make the essence shift: I relax even further and become aware of the vast, open sky of consciousness that is in the background of all my thoughts and feelings. Because I had been lost in my thoughts, I had not been feeling connected to the pure consciousness that flows through everything. At the moment I made the shift to feeling the consciousness—the essence—I felt free. Freedom is being in touch with the sky that holds everything, and as I saw through the clouds I realized the sky had been there all along.

This is the essence shift. It happens the moment you drop your attachment to a particular part of consciousness and shift your attention to consciousness itself. This shift takes precedence for a reason. We can see why, using the emotion of anger as an example. Until we shift from anger to essence, anger is bigger than we are. It has us. We are in the grip of it. The moment we shift to essence, we have the anger, but it doesn't have us. Our essence is bigger than it. The difference is immense, and it affects every aspect of human life.

Let me share a snippet of conversation with you. It is one of several thousand I have saved over the years. I save them because they illustrate an important point better than anything I could invent.

ME: I notice your hand touching your chest. Tune in to what you're feeling there.

DORIE (a twenty-eight-year-old internist in the last year of her residency): My hand? Oh, yes. Umm, I'm feeling a constriction, a pressure . . . around my lungs.

ME: And as you tune in to that, do you notice an emotion that you could name?

DORIE: (pause) I feel the loss of Edward. I had so much tied up in making it work. Now I know it will never work. My mind knows this, but my heart still aches.

ME: Face into the sadness. Let it breathe.

DORIE: (Cries for several moments.) It's hard.

ME: I know.

DORIE: And yet I know it's right.

ME: Yes, probably so, but let your body know it's okay to grieve. You had a lot of expectations of this relationship, and when those collapse your body reacts strongly.

DORIE: (Takes a big breath.) Yeah. You know, it's strange but I feel happy at the same time.

ME: Tell me about that.

DORIE: Well, all around the sadness I feel kind of a glow, like the sadness is resting in something bigger.

ME: Ahhh, yes. Probably because you let yourself feel your sadness, you can feel all the open space that's there all the time.

An Experiment to Try Right Now

Try the essence shift with me right now. You can make this shift anytime; it takes only a second. Notice any feeling or body sensation. Right now I am tuning in to a feeling of fullness in my stomach, probably the result of the oat bran pancake I ate a half hour ago. As I let my awareness rest on the sensation, I feel more details of it. It is more to the left than to the right, and it is really not a solid sensation as it seemed at first. It is really made up of tiny waves.

Let your attention rest on the sensation you have chosen, and really stay with it for a while. Find out what you can learn from it.

Now I notice some guilt and fear. I am losing some weight in preparation for an upcoming television show, and I am scared that I have sabotaged my program. I take a deep breath and let the out-breath go with a whoosh.

As my awareness deepens, I feel a warmth and spaciousness behind and beyond the surface sensations. The essence is there, the backdrop of everything. As I tune in to it, the sensation of fullness actually shifts, becomes more pleasant. I suspect it is because everything feels more at ease when welcomed into essence.

To make the essence shift is to acknowledge a feeling or thought but not get caught in it and take it for real. How much happier human beings would be if we knew how to make this simple shift! If we knew how to see that our thoughts are just thoughts and that our feelings are just feelings, we would be better able to live consciously. We would see that ninety-nine times out of a hundred, our thoughts are merely reflections of the mood we happen to be in. They are not to be taken seriously as accurate reflections of reality. They are certainly not to be acted upon.

I saw this so clearly one day on a bike ride. In the first twenty minutes of the ride I pedaled by a colleague's house on my way up into the mountains. I was fresh, the morning air was crisp and exhilarating, and I was excited about getting out into the mountains. As I whizzed past his house, I had a positive flurry of thoughts about my colleague. I thought about several good contributions he had made to his field and how glad I was he had found happiness in a second marriage. After passing his house, I thought no further about him until I came back four hours later. Now, after a rigorous ride, I was dog tired, hungry, feeling a slight headache, and in a hurry to get home. As I passed his house, I had another flurry of thoughts about him, but this time the tone was completely different. I thought about what an unpleasant woman his new wife was, how sorry I felt for him that he couldn't seem to see it, and how wrong he was to have voted opposite to me on a number of campus issues. When I caught the tone of these thoughts, I had to laugh. The only thing that had changed was my mood. He had not changed at all, and what's more, he probably wasn't even home. Because I was tired, I saw him, his marriage, and his contribution to the university through a negative filter. My thoughts were simply mirroring how I felt inside.

I'm glad I know how our minds work in this regard. I was able to make an essence shift and feel good instead of giving a home to this unproductive line of thought. After noticing the sour nature of my thought stream, I stepped out of it onto the shore and watched it go by. Imagine the progress that would be made in peace talks if our political leaders were skilled in making the essence shift. Imagine how much happier we would all be if we knew this simple fact about how thoughts work.

The essence shift begins with an undefended willingness to place your attention on unarguable reality. That sentence contains a lot of distilled wisdom, so let's look at each piece of it separately.

What is "undefended willingness"? Come into a therapy session with me while I show you what it is and what it is not. A heated discussion is going on between Joyce and Leo. They are racing for the victim position, blaming each other for a passel of wrongdoings. I interrupt them in midsentence:

ME: Pause for a moment right where you are. (They look at me like two deer caught in the headlights, so surprised are they.) Just take a breath. (They stop and take a breath.)

ME: Stop arguing for a moment, and put your attention on something unarguable that's going on in your body. Tell a truth that the other person can't argue about. I know from long experience that no one ever solved a problem by blaming the other person.

LEO: (irritably) Huh?

JOYCE: (looking at her watch) He doesn't understand.

Our personalities are revealed by how we resist the unflinching look at reality. I have asked them to say something true. Instead, she gets confused, looks at her watch, and touches her hair. His personality is based in part on defending against reality by being irritable; hers is based on playing dumb and attending to vanity. Shopping is a major sport for her, competitive tennis for him. They argue endlessly about both.

ME: I notice when I ask you to shift your consciousness into your body, to stop arguing and focus on reality, you each do something to avoid my suggestion. Leo, you looked at me irritably and said "Huh?" Joyce, you looked confused, glanced at your watch, rearranged your hair.

I have two purposes in making this observation. I want to point out what one of my mentors called "the elusive obvious." They have been doing this particular dance so long they truly do not see what everyone else sees: it's not making them happy. I want to feed it back to them so they can see it. Second, I want them to get angry at me, at least for a moment, to have them form an alliance by being mad at someone other than each other. They are quick to oblige.

LEO: How come you're suddenly doing all this nit-picking?

JOYCE: Aren't we about out of time? I don't want to spend all our time on this.

They both get mad at me for blowing the whistle on this unconscious game. Many people think their survival is threatened if they put their attention on the world of pain—physical, emotional, and spiritual—in their bodies. They will resist doing so by many means, including attacking the messenger who brings the news. I actually saw one man fall stone asleep the moment he was asked to tune in to an emotion in his body. Ordinarily—at a party or on the tennis court—we don't point out one another's defensive moves. However, in therapy we are not in an ordinary situation; the clock is ticking away at three dollars a minute, and it would be malpractice on my part if I did not intervene in their destructive game. So I invite them to enter the body, and I stand back to see what happens.

After a few defensive skirmishes, they do what I asked them to do, to let go and focus attention inward. Now the game is over. They are in the world of the real. Leo confronts his pain about his father's departure when he was nine. He realizes that his whole personality—his hostility, his obsessive neatness, his misplaced rage at his wife—comes out of the unfaced agony of abandonment. Joyce opens up to her sadness and her anger about a host of losses. They go down through layers of pain and grit until they feel the essence that is at the bottom of every sincere inquiry into ourselves.

At the end of the session they hold hands, in touch with essence and allies in the journey of conscious living. They have beheld what they thought was the worst in themselves and found that it was made only of mind stuff. Now they can turn their attention to what they want to create instead of eating up their creative energy in endless dramas of persecution and victimhood.

The Truth Shift:
The Choice to Reveal Your Authentic Self

A second powerful shift does much to create your destiny. Dozens of times a day you are faced with a question, and the question is this: do I tell the truth or not? Human beings often withhold telling the truth about three key things. The act of withholding the truth in these areas destroys our happiness and shapes our destiny toward misfortune. By contrast, these same things hold the key to our liberation, if we can learn to speak frankly and easily about them. They are: facts, feelings, and fantasies.

The most common fact that comes up in sessions: you have done something you feel guilty about, and you haven't told the significant person about it.

The most common feelings: you are mad about something or sad or scared or joyful, and you haven't given yourself the ten seconds of pure attention to it that will allow it (and most feelings) to resolve. In other words, you haven't told yourself the full truth about it, and you haven't told the relevant other person or persons. This act of lying to yourself and others puts a wobble in your whole being that can only be smoothed out through full communication. We are a living stream of feelings, day in and day out, and the only issue is whether we speak about them openly or hide them. Hide them from yourself, and you are numb and riddled with symptoms. Hide them from others, and no one knows you. Speak about them openly, and your life is lived in waves of authenticity and intimacy.

One of the most common fantasies I hear: you keep cycling a thought through your mind about your sexual attraction to someone. You haven't fully acknowledged the attraction to yourself, and you haven't told the other person about it. Or you have a fantasy that someone doesn't like you. You don't talk to the person about it, and soon you find yourself thinking negatively about the other person.

If you notice carefully, you will discover which facts, feelings, and fantasies are the ones that need to be communicated. The crucial ones will usually keep recycling until you handle them or drown them out in some way. Trouble is, they don't stay drowned, coming back to haunt us in one way or another for a long, long time. The only way out is through speaking the truth. The moment we open our mouths to speak, though, we face another crucial moment of choice.

The Purpose Shift: Knowing Your Intention

Next time you are in a situation that is not going well, take the following bold step: inquire into what your purpose is at the moment. I've done it hundreds of times, and each time I've been richly rewarded for the move (although at the time I haven't always liked what I've seen about myself). I might be in the middle of some conversation, when I feel my muscles tighten and a slight ringing begins in my ears. This cues me that something is wrong. In the old days, before I caught on to telling the no-blame truth and taking personal responsibility, I would usually assume it was the other person's problem. Now, though, I've learned to make the inward moves we've discussed: What truth am I withholding? Can I let go of blame? What is my purpose at the moment? Often, I am humbled by realizing that my purpose at the moment is nothing more than to be right. Knowing this, though, allows me the possibility of shifting my intention to harmony and resolution.

Purpose is a powerful inquiry. If we ask sincerely, from a place of wonder instead of justification, we can work miracles with the tiniest of shifts. Imagine, for example, that you are caught up in an argument with a loved one. You are pitching hot words back and forth at each other, and nothing is getting resolved. Suddenly you pause and wonder: what is my purpose at the moment? In a rush, you realize that you are acting out of an unconscious purpose. Because of your painful conditioning history, your purpose is to make the person wrong, to cause hurt, to get sympathy, or to avoid intimacy because you don't feel like you deserve it. These are all purposes rooted in your upbringing and your relationship history, but you consciously no longer want to operate out of them. They have a powerful pull, though, and you are only human. You take a deep breath and shift to a conscious purpose of your own choosing: to feel good and contribute to the good feeling of your loved one.

You say, "I got carried away. I hurt, and I wanted you to hurt, too. I need your support right now, but I don't feel like I deserve anyone's love. Let's start all over." You remember your purpose and say, "Let's figure out what we need to do to restore harmony here and now."

When we open our mouths to communicate something of emotional significance, we speak with one of two intentions: the intention to be right or the intention to be in harmony. The intention to be right comes burdened with justification and defensiveness. The intention to be in harmony releases defensiveness and carries with it no need to justify.

John opens his mouth to communicate his irritation with Sylvia. When he intends to be right, it comes out like this:

JOHN: You didn't pick up Kevin on time from soccer yesterday. Why don't you ever keep a single agreement you make? Don't you care about these kids?

Notice the prevalence of *yous*. There is no intention to be in harmony or actually to solve the problem. It's about blame.

If he intended to be in harmony, it would come out quite differently:

JOHN: You didn't pick up Kevin on time from soccer yesterday. I felt afraid when he called. I was worried something had happened to

> you. I also felt angry that it had happened again for the second time this month.

Here, he says what happened and how he felt. It's unarguable—it's not about being right but about restoring harmony.

I have seen thousands of communications like these in my office over the years. It's a tough challenge to get people to switch their intentions from being right to being in harmony. I have always been amazed at how attached we human beings are to being right. It's especially frustrating for me because I've had a lot of practice. I can shift out of being right much quicker now than twenty years ago, but I still get stuck from time to time. When I'm in a communication warp with somebody, letting go of being right often feels like having a tooth extracted. I know it's going to feel better after I let go, but part of me resists it.

Defensiveness destroys communication. I watch a scene play out in the therapy office time and again.

> WIFE: You look angry. (His face is red, his fists are clenched, his breath is short and sharp. A team of impartial observers would unanimously agree that this person is angry.)
>
> HUSBAND: Not at all. I'm feeling just fine.

Who does he think he's fooling? Unfortunately, it's only himself. After a few intense minutes of backing and filling, he comes out and tells her what he's angry about. Meanwhile, life has been ticking by as he ran through his defensive moves. How easy it would be if we simply came out and said how we felt with no defensiveness! After all, who in the world, besides him, cares if he is angry?

Nothing real ever needs to be defended, but I've seen many people expend enormous, life-costing energy defending it anyway.

The Integrity Shift: Freedom Through Healthy Responsibility

In every significant life situation we are faced with a fourth choice: to take full responsibility for an issue or to blame someone else. Each time we avoid responsibility, we claim victimhood. We claim to be the victim of our wife or boyfriend or co-worker or the world itself. We say, "I am powerless in the face of my body, my IQ, the past, the injustices of the world." We argue for our limitations, and, sure enough, we get to keep them.

Blame is a dominant theme of our time. Jockeying for the victim position consumes an enormous amount of TV time and newspaper space. Turn on a daytime talk show, and you are likely to see sullen people yelling self-righteously at each other about how they've been wronged. Flip to the slower-paced world of soap opera, and you will see endless dramas of victimhood and recrimination, choreographed in torpid eight-minute minuets between commercials for pain relievers. Watch the news shows like *60 Minutes*, and you will see story after story about victims and those who are to blame for victimizing them.

Why are victim dramas so popular and compelling? I think it may now be wired into our nervous systems; after all, most of us come from centuries of oppression. I believe it takes an evolutionary shift to move beyond the fascination with story lines based on victimhood. Perhaps the fascination is based on a chemical addiction to the adrenaline rush you get in the race for the victim position. There is great glee to be had in the finger pointing of blame. At the moment of being right, we can forget about all our other problems. The electric glee of self-righteousness gives us a clear view (or so we think) of what is causing our problems. We saw this at its extreme in Nazi Germany, where the Nazis most definitely thought they were the victims of the Jews, no matter how it looked from the outside. We see a miniature version of the same problem in every argument between people, no matter how trivial. I have been privy to petty squabbles between couples and titanic arguments in corporate boardrooms. In every case there is a mad dash for the victim position. Each side thinks the other is the perpetrator. We seem never to tire of the story.

Taking responsibility is a quieter pleasure, a freedom and a joy rather than a glee. When we encounter the moment in which we can choose to take healthy responsibility or claim the victim position, we stand at a doorway to the infinite. Indeed, we face the possibility of genuine happiness. And we must ask ourselves, are we ready for that? The teacher Gurdjieff once said that he had found the addiction to suffering to be the hardest of all to cure. Long after the cocaine, the liquor, and the tobacco are put away, we must face our insistence that life can be hard.

It's a snap anywhere in the world to get up a conversation about how bad things are and how much we are being victimized by the forces in the world. But just try to get one going about the joys of taking healthy responsibility. Start a conversation with, "Isn't it great how easy our lives become once we take responsibility for them?" Be prepared for a stampede of people backpedaling away from you. This conversation takes the courage to look unflinchingly at how life actually works. It takes the courage to move beyond defensiveness to a heartfelt inquiry into conscious living. A conversation about genuine, healthy responsibility requires being more fascinated with the unfolding of creative possibilities in yourself and others than you are with the perpetuating of your victim status. Tough talk, perhaps, but I've learned all this the hard way, and I'd want you to be equally straightforward with me if you had this information.

As people master responsibility, I notice that they eventually take responsibility for the world itself. They see that they create the world through their actions and their interpretations of the world, and both their actions and their interpretations can be changed. For example, you may, as I did, dream up the world as a place of scarcity. I come from a background of impoverishment in both love and money. Not only were these things scarce, but stories were told to support and justify their scarcity. Eventually, though, I saw that I must take responsibility for how I constructed the world. If it was not to my liking, who but me would change it? So I eliminated conversations about scarcity from my life, to the best of my ability. I put myself on a "negativity diet" for a year, where I vowed not to speak of my limitations with regard to anything. I would speak only of possibility, and I would interrupt those who tried to engage me in conversations about victimhood. I came to see what Epictetus had pointed out two thousand years ago: it is not the events of life that are bothersome or hurtful, it is the way we think about them.

I made up a new world for myself, one in which there was plenty of love and money. To my amazement, plenty of both flowed into my life. Had they been there all the time, waiting for me to turn on the tap? I'll never know, but I don't really care, either. All that matters to me now, as then, is that I live in a different world as a result of changing my interpretations of it. William James said over a hundred years ago that the greatest psychological discovery of his time was this: that human beings could change the outer circumstances of their lives by changing their attitudes of mind. I have made that same discovery in my world, and I urge you to experiment with it in yours.

Ultimately, the shift to personal responsibility is what I call a "wonder move." You make the shift from knowing who's to blame to wondering about what has caused the situation. A powerful wonder move is from "Why is the world treating me like this?" to "How have I arranged it so I'm having this experience?" There is genuine likelihood of transformation in this move, because you shift from the zone of the known, where there is no possibility, to the zone of the unknown, where there is infinite possibility. Once you have let go of knowing who is to blame, you are free to wonder about how things came to be the way they are.

The Action Shift: The Choice to Act or Let Be

The first four shifts clear the way for you to take effective action. The question, though, is, which things do you take action about, and which do you let rest? I notice that every day I am faced with one path of action after another. Which path do you take, and which do you leave untrodden? The Stoics were very clear about this key issue, and I have earlier quoted the succinct wisdom of Epictetus: "The secret of happiness is knowing that there are some things you can control and some things you cannot."

If there is an action that can be taken, our bodies poise to take it until we decide not to act. Then we can relax. A simple example is the common problems of headache and back pain. Research by specialists such as John Sarno, M.D., shows clearly that most back pain derives from unacknowledged and unexpressed anger. The muscles of the back and neck poise for action when there is a trespass of some kind. Whether this trespass is real (a person standing too close in an elevator) or imaginary (replaying an argument in your mind) does not seem to matter. The muscles in the back and neck stand to attention in anticipation of acting to resolve the trespass. All animals have the same mechanism built in from hundreds of thousands of years ago. In the cat or dog, the "trespass" wiring can be seen easily because the fur stands up along the pathway of those particular muscles. You see the hackles of a dog rise, and you know at a glance that it's experiencing a trespass.

What causes our back pain or headache, then? Why don't dogs and cats get them? The answer is simple yet profoundly useful. We get the back pain because we don't take the required action and we don't consciously choose to let it go. If a dog is napping in the front lawn and hears footsteps, it awakens with its hackles at attention. Trespass! But then it recognizes that it's the same old mailman from times past, and it chooses not to take the action. The hackles relax, and the dog goes back to sleep.

In *our* lives, however, the problems are complicated by the social realities in which we live. Our boss calls us in and chews us out for fifteen minutes about something. Our hackles stand at attention; our biological desire, carefully honed and supremely useful in jungle and savanna, is to lash out or get out. In the modern work environment, though, it is not considered socially appropriate to punch out or run out or curl up into a ball in the corner.

So we sit there and take it. Unless we can muster a socially appropriate action or consciously release the tension in some way, we may go home with a headache or a pain in the back.

The choice is to take an action or to find a way to let our bodies and minds relax without taking action.

This moment of choice runs through every day of our lives. Here are two more examples.

You have a conflict with a relative. You know you should pick up the phone and work it out, but you just can't seem to bring yourself to do it. You don't take the action, and you don't let it go. You stew and hurt and worry.

You lose some money on a stock that plummets right after you buy it. Your friend and neighbor across the street gave you the tip. You have the urge to tell him you're angry, but you don't because his daughter baby-sits for you every Saturday night. Besides, you tell yourself, you were the one who acted on the tip. So you don't take action, and you don't let it go, either. You find yourself still thinking about it weeks later.

An Experiment to Try Right Now

Apply this principle to something important in your life. Focus on an issue that is prominent in your life right now. Pick one that would really make a difference if you experienced a shift in it. Once you have selected one, ask yourself: is this within my power to change? If you answer yes, ask another question: do I want to put energy into changing it? If you can change it and you want to put energy into it, do it.

If the answer is no to one or the other of those questions, your task is to let it alone. There is no other choice. If you cannot change it or you don't want to expend the energy to change it, you have to let it be. You need all your energy to change the things you can change. And even then, you have to pick your projects with utmost care. Human beings are finite and have only energy for a few big projects at a time. You may not be able to lose fifty pounds, finish your Ph.D., take care of your aging parent, and write a symphony all in the same year. One of my clients was trying to do all of those things at the same time plus help her son get off drugs. It was the latter project that overloaded her circuits and caused everything to fall apart in her life.

I have worked with hundreds of people who were in a close relationship with an addict. The more they focused on the other person's addiction, the worse the situation seemed to get. We don't really have any control over other people. It is not up to me whether you drink or not. You can't control whether I take a drug, whether it's a sip of coffee or a puff of smoke. Only I have control over whether I do it or not. The moment we acknowledge we are powerless over other people, we are free to do two things. We can let go completely, freeing others to learn their own lessons. Or we can consciously choose to mount an influence campaign. If we choose to influence, we need to approach it like a business arrangement. We need to have a goal and a plan along with the commitment to carry it through to completion.

Most people don't do it that way, though. They stay in the unconscious zone, wishing the other person would change but not really making a clear plan to accomplish it. The wheels spin, and nothing ever changes.

The AA program hinges on the shift I am describing. There alcoholics admit powerlessness over alcohol, saying, "I have no control over my alcoholism." Up until then, they thought they could manage it. They thought their egos were big enough to walk away from it. But guess what? The ego that thinks it's big enough to walk away from alcohol is that same one that requires drinking to quiet it! Thinking we can change the unchangeable is the cunning trick the ego plays on us to allow it to stay in control. Once alcoholics admit that they cannot change this fact of themselves, they can focus on something that really counts: whether or not they take a drink this day.

This moment, this day, you are facing a number of choices and actions. Pick one that is within your control. Pick one that is the very next thing that needs to be done. Do it—no matter how large or small—and watch the magic that unfolds from this move.

The Us Shift: From Ego Centeredness to Connection

In the Us Shift, I move from being concerned with my own needs to being concerned with the empowerment of others and the well-being of the community. This is a shift I was unaware of until I was thirty-five, for in my twenties and early thirties I was so bent on my own goals and visions that I did not stop to concern myself with others. Then one day I had a wake-up moment.

When I was thirty-five I took a sabbatical and trekked through Europe and Asia. It was the sort of trip I had dreamed of making when I was in my late teens, but life and I conspired to keep me from doing it until a number of years later. On my journey I stayed for several days at a remote hermitage in the foothills of the Himalayas. One morning I sat on the riverbank and watched a swarm of teenaged day laborers from a nearby village as they carried out a project. Each carried a heavy stone up a steep hill to where the local guru was supervising the construction of a temple. When a boy would get to the top, he would drop the stone and return down the hill to pick up another. This continued for hours. Upon inquiry, I found that each boy was being paid one rupee (about a dime) per day for the job. When I heard this I was dumbstruck and depressed, because there were dozens more who had not been picked for the job. The stone carriers felt lucky, and their passed-over friends squatted nearby all day, looking on with envy.

As I watched all this from the opposite riverbank, I felt a deep despair steal over me. I realized that this was probably going to be the way life was for these kids and likely for their kids, too. Is this what it's all about? I wondered. We carry a rock up a hill, then come down and get another one—if we're lucky? We eke out a living or a hardscrabble existence for our seventy years and then are gone in wink of an eye? What's the point?

I sat back and breathed into the pain. I felt waves of despair for all the unused potential that died within us every day in a thousand ways. I felt grief for the boys and felt shame that I could not help them. I stayed with those feelings as the minutes stretched on. After a while, I felt a shift in consciousness wash over me. Suddenly there was no "my" pain and "their" pain. We became one single pain—me and the boys and the collective pain in the world—and then we became one pulsing organism, always yearning for ways to express our potential. Beneath the pain was the yearning, and beneath that was the pure coursing energy of existence. The more I opened up to the feelings, the more they transformed into essence. I could feel the energy and space of the universe flowing through everything and attached to nothing. The nothing at the center of everything was my own essence, the essence of the boys, and the essence of the whole of creation. At a certain moment there became no "me" separate from anything; I had become "us."

I felt a rush of ecstasy in this moment. I reveled in it for twenty or thirty minutes, then the sweet feeling began to subside. As I came down from the high of the experience, the same boys were trudging up the same hill, but everything looked different to me. They were simply doing what they were doing, and I was simply doing what I was doing. That was that, and this is it.

I realized in that moment that my sojourn was over. It was time for me to go back to my own world and make a difference in the singular way I could. There was little or nothing I could do to improve the lives of the boys on the hill, but there were contributions I could make to my own community through my own skills. The trouble was, I had been making my contributions from a sense of "me," not from a sense of "us." The shift changed everything in me. Now I was committed to *our* world, not *my* world.

That moment was the first time I was aware of the us shift; since then I have felt it many times. It often comes in moments of polarization. I will be in conflict with someone, and pained emotions will fill the air. Then suddenly I feel a shift to "usness," and the conflict dissolves. There is a brotherhood and sisterhood where before there was a wall.

I have witnessed the us shift with many polarized elements of the community. I've facilitated sessions on some of the most emotionally charged ground in the world, such as inside barracks at Birkenau and Auschwitz in the dead of winter. I've worked with Bosnians and Serbs, Arabs and Jews, Irish Protestants and Catholics—and I have been deeply moved to see people all over the world shift from conflict to a sense of "us." To watch pacifists and army colonels embrace in that space of "usness" has given me an unshakable optimism in the future.

The Ultimate Shift: From Anything to Love

I've been showered with blessings every time I have made a shift from anything to love. Any shift will do—from fear to love, from logic to love, from hatred to love. All we have to do is catch ourselves in the act of doing something stupid or ugly or foolish or painful, and love ourselves anyway. All we have to do is catch someone else in the act of behaving in some way we don't like, and love them anyway. Boundaries may need to be set, of course; that's part of love, too. If children are leaving the refrigerator door open, we may need to instruct them in the ways of refrigerator etiquette. Studies show that 85 percent of our messages to children are negative: "Don't!" "Stop!" "How could you?" Here is where love can help us immensely. If we shift to loving our children before we tell them not to leave the refrigerator door open, our lessons seem to get through to them much more deeply. Perhaps more important, each time we shift from anger to love or fear to love or even acceptance to love, we lubricate the ultimate hinge of consciousness, a hinge that has squeaked badly for a long, long time.

The ultimate skill of conscious living is to have the hinge of consciousness so thoroughly oiled that we can shift in any moment from the contracted clench of fear to the open-handed, openhearted embrace of love. Fear sucks the belly in; love lets it go. Fear makes a fist; love lets it go. This is why the journey of conscious living is so rich: the possibility exists in every interaction—whether with another person or in the vast spaces of ourselves—to come from fear or from love. It's always a dance on the edge of who we are and who we can be. That is why I think of conscious living as the infinite journey, and why I recommend it so highly to any questing spirit.

PART 2

The Real World

Conscious Solutions to Timeless Problems of Living

Now that we've explored the key concepts of conscious living, it's time to put them to work in the real world we face every day. When you wake up in the morning, you get up to face the same problems human beings have awakened to for the past few thousand years. We're more likely to get a full stomach than our ancestors, but can any of us be sure of going into the day with full self-esteem? We may go to work in the comfort of a minivan, but are we any more likely to work in harmony with our colleagues than our ancestors who commuted by chariot?

In other words, certain problems of living have been with us for a long time, regardless of improvements in technology. Indeed, technology may even make some of our problems worse. Are we better or worse off when a dictator can use the power of television to broadcast his message? Are we better or worse off when a teenager can download bomb-making instructions from the Internet?

In 1995 I surveyed several thousand people to find out the areas of living in which they most needed clear information. The question was: "If a school existed that taught what you really need to know for a successful and happy life, what subjects would it teach?"

Four areas were deemed crucial:

- *Self-esteem, the art of discovering who you really are and expressing it in the world.*
- *How to attract a mate or partner with whom you could resonate and grow over time.*
- *How to navigate the problems of living and loving together over time.*
- *How to create a life, career, and lifestyle of your own design rather than relying on the roles and maps of the past.*

In 1998 the Foundation for Twenty-First Century Leadership, a nonprofit organization founded by Kathlyn and me, launched The Living University to offer courses on these and other areas. We have now trained nearly one hundred faculty members, who offer the courses in their home communities. The response has been encouraging, and we plan to keep training approximately one hundred new faculty a year. We have faculty now in the U.S., Canada, Latin America, Europe, Japan, and Israel.

Here in part 2, I offer these courses to you in written form. The material in this section is exactly what you would hear and see in the lectures that are part of The Living University courses. You will notice that the writing style differs from the style in part 1. That's because I'm trying to preserve the fast-paced, informal feel of the lectures. In addition, the courses in The Living University contain experiential activities that bring the ideas to life. The most essential activities are included in this section, and I urge you to take the time to work through them on the spot. If you do, you'll greatly enhance your understanding of the core concepts of conscious living.

Without further ado, let's begin with the most fundamental of all problems of conscious living: discovering who we really are.

CHAPTER 5

The Foundation of Self-Esteem

Discovering Who You Are

All of us need to know who we really are. Knowing ourselves is the first step toward feeling organically good inside. If we're out of touch with our feelings and our needs—not to mention grander issues like soul and essence and life purpose—we don't feel good. If we can't feel good by natural means, we're ripe for the picking by the cult leader, the gang lord, the advertising industry, and the drug seller—the one who operates the corner drugstore or the one who operates on the street corner itself.

Discovering who you truly are is the only way to find and keep a permanent sense of self-esteem. Only a deep and thorough knowledge of ourselves will give us the unshakable sense of self that can stand up to the rigors of life in the twenty-first century.

A Paradox

Self-esteem rests on a remarkable paradox: we can give to others effectively only when we love ourselves deeply, and we can love ourselves deeply only when we contribute to others fully. Self-esteem is like breathing: if you breathe all the way in, you can breathe all the way out. If you breathe out fully, you can breathe back in again fully. When we take a full breath of love for ourselves, we can contribute to others without depleting our own energy. And when we can give completely to others, we can take in a full breath of new energy for ourselves.

Imagine a person walking toward you, someone who's really important to you. Now picture two very different moves on your part. In scene one, you fold your arms across your chest and turn away from the person, refusing to make loving contact. In scene two, you throw open your arms wide, smile lovingly, and embrace the person.

Now imagine that the one you're embracing is yourself. Notice how you would feel if you turned your back on yourself, as many of us do. Now imagine how you would feel if you truly, genuinely embraced yourself in love.

For this reason, who you are and how you feel about yourself inside are the first required courses of life. Self-esteem is paramount, for if we are out of harmony with ourselves, we will contribute to disharmony everywhere. A moment of heartfelt and humble self-love can shift our evolutionary journey to warp speed.

Everything we really need to know about self-esteem comes down to six secrets. We will cover the first three in this chapter and the remaining three in the next chapter.

- Loving yourself without conditions
- Living in integrity
- Distinguishing your essence from your personas
- Handling fear
- Expressing your creative potential
- Developing emotional literacy

In other words, we need to ask ourselves the following questions:

Can I love myself unconditionally? If I can love myself, I open the possibility of loving others the same way. If I cannot love myself, there is no possibility of loving others.

Am I living in integrity? If I am, I can hold myself in high regard. If I am not, I cannot feel good no matter what I accomplish in the external world.

Can I make my true home in essence—my inner core of pure consciousness—rather than in the outer world of my feelings, my thoughts, or the social masks I wear? If I can, I award myself the great gift of a conscious life, the deep and unshakable feeling of well-being that flows only from feeling our deepest connection with ourselves and the universe around us.

Are my fears limiting me? Can I break free of the bonds of fear to rise to my highest potential? Am I bringing forth my creativity? If you are reaching down inside yourself and bringing your creative impulses to light, your self-esteem will grow daily. It doesn't matter if your creative product is a poem, a symphony, a happy marriage, or a tureen of transcendental clam chowder. All that matters is that we commit ourselves to full expression and are taking action on our creative projects.

Am I contributing to others in a way that fills me with energy? If not—if the way I give to others depletes me—my contributions will not genuinely serve others. Our gifts reach their destinations only when we give them in a way that empowers both ourselves and the receivers.

If your answer is yes to these questions, your self-esteem will flourish and you will feel fine even when you don't feel good. Genuine self-esteem makes a welcome space for both positive and negative feelings so that you will be able to feel good about yourself even when things are not going well.

Fortunately for all of us, self-esteem does not require a perfect yes to any of the core questions. Self-esteem is a flowing process, not a granite rock. It's made of tiny moves along the way, not of arriving at a particular place. We simply need to be in the process of feeling essence, learning to love ourselves, developing integrity, and expressing our creative potential.

Daring to Dream

The biggest problem of self-esteem is this: when our self-esteem is low, we don't even realize we have a self-esteem problem. We think that's just the way life is.

Let me give you an example from my own life. One symptom of poor self-esteem is that you doubt that you can fulfill your dreams and visions. In your heart you know you will never get to where you want to go. A second symptom goes much deeper, to the very core of ourselves: we do not dare to dream at all. There is no vision of what we could become, because there is no real self—no us—to become. I know both of these symptoms well.

At this point in my life I would be regarded as a success by almost anyone. I have a beautiful, loving, and brilliant wife who is my creative partner as well. My children are grown and engaged in their lives, I am blessed with abundance, a satisfying measure of worldly recognition, good health, and a house by the sea. Yet I sometimes still find myself doubting that I can fulfill my dreams. My visions are big and nearly always accompanied by doubt. I find my edge almost every day.

I sometimes have trouble accepting this part of the process. I once thought self-esteem was something that happened in a whoosh and that was that. If I had good self-esteem I would always be brimming with confidence. Now I know this is nonsense.

Self-esteem is living in such a state of creative expansion that you go over your edge every day. You are always living in wonder about whether you can do it or not. More creativity means more doubt. Yet you keep breathing, keep moving, keep creating. You breathe through the doubt and ride a bigger wave of creativity.

My self-esteem was once so low that I didn't even dare to dream. I grew up in an impoverished Southern family that was plagued by addiction and other dramas. I might have gone down the same path had it not been for Dixie Jean Allen, who jump-started me as a dreamer. One day I was walking down the hall as a high school junior when Miss Allen flagged me down. She was my guidance counselor, but until then I was only on nodding terms with her.

"What are your college plans?" she asked.

Looking down at the floor, I mumbled that my mother was going through hard times and that, at best, I might enroll for courses at the county's junior college. But I really wasn't even sure we could afford that. Miss Allen's mouth dropped open. She looked dumbfounded. She took me into her office and sat me down.

"Have you ever considered applying for a scholarship to a good college or university?" she asked.

Now it was my turn to be dumbfounded. I had heard only of football scholarships, and that's what I thought she meant.

"No," I said, "I'm just not good enough to play college football." This was an accurate assessment on my part, not a statement of poor self-esteem. When I was in the tenth grade my history teacher, who was also the football coach, said, "Son, you're big. How come you ain't out for football?"

If I'd had my wits about me, my reply would have been, "Because I'm a pudgy intellectual with absolutely no athletic skills." However, I was a teenage boy without a father in a neighborhood where everybody else had one. I was hungry for attention from a male authority figure, so hungry I had no idea that it gnawed at me. So what I actually said was, "Sign me up." I ended up playing football for my last two years of high school, during which I played on a team that racked up the longest losing streak in the school's history. We were dismal, and I contributed my fair share to our pathetic record. I also hurt my knee, the pain of which I can sometimes still feel when I get out of bed.

Miss Allen shook her head, looking somewhat exasperated. "I'm talking about academic scholarships."

I said I had never heard about such a thing. When she explained how it worked, I could hardly believe it.

"You mean, I could get my college paid for by just making good grades?"

I realize how stupid this sounds now, but that's just how little I knew.

"Sure," she said. "You made one of the highest scores in the region on the aptitude tests. You could get a scholarship just about anywhere. Certainly to the University of Florida or Florida State, but there are even better possibilities. An alumni of an Ivy League school who lives in the area called me about you and wants to meet you."

Fast-forward to a day in winter of my senior year. Miss Allen came flying down the hall to where I was standing near my locker.

She had a letter in her hand, informing her that I had won a scholarship to my highest choice school. That afternoon, walking home from school, I noticed there was something different about me, but I couldn't figure out just what. Suddenly I realized it was my hands. They were relaxed and open, compared to the clenched fists I'd held ever since I could remember. There must have been a part of me that was afraid I would never escape. Now I had my ticket out, and I was free.

Yale seemed too big a stretch, in a different galaxy from where I lived. I ended up going to Rollins, an excellent liberal arts college less than fifty miles from home. My ostensible reason for choosing to stay near home was that I was concerned about my grandmother's health. She was approaching eighty, and I wanted to be near her in her final years. Looking back on it, though, I now realize it was my low self-esteem, as well as my love for my grandmother, that kept me from going north to an Ivy League school.

Almost thirty years later I met Miss Allen quite by chance at a funeral and had the opportunity to thank her for changing my life. Her concern for developing my potential inspired me in the direction of a career in the helping professions and to a lifelong passion for helping people (and myself) confront our limiting beliefs about ourselves. My wondering about this subject led me through labyrinths in myself and others that I never imagined could exist. One dark and unexplored place in ourselves is when and where we cease to love ourselves.

It All Comes Down to a Special Kind of Love

Self-esteem ultimately is about whether you can love yourself and others unconditionally. If we don't love ourselves, we will always be chasing it from others. If our feelings toward ourselves are flavored with guilt and criticism, our love toward others will be contaminated by these same flavors. A special kind of love is required, and it must be directed toward ourselves before it can be adequately expressed to others.

Love is the antidote to fear. Fear pulls us into contraction, but love allows us to expand again. When we don't know how to love ourselves, we live in that state of contraction permanently. Fear is not only a fist around our stomachs; it grips out hearts as well. Loving ourselves is the only way out of the grip of fear.

Loving yourself is not about conceit. Conceit is an attempt to prove to others that you're lovable when you've decided inside that you really aren't. Loving yourself is also not false humility. True love for ourselves is the ultimate acknowledgment of equality. It says, "I am here and you are here and we are all equals in this universe." Conceit says, "I am here at your expense," while false humility says, "You are here at mine." Genuine love for ourselves celebrates ourselves in seamless union with the whole of everything. As to the how-to, there isn't one. All we can do is to love ourselves as much as we can from wherever we are.

Would you, this moment, give yourself a heartbeat or two of this pure love?

Living in Integrity

If you are not feeling good, if you're not feeling loving toward yourself, there is one incredibly obvious place to look, but almost nobody remembers to look there. If I could afford it, I'd fly a banner through the sky over every city and town with the following piece of information on it. I'd run a commercial every hour and have it printed on the side of milk cartons. Here's the message:

When you're not feeling good, don't look back into the past to find the reason. Don't look to what you ate or what you dreamed last night. Look right where you are, at any place where you're out of integrity. In order to love yourself unconditionally, you need to be operating with integrity. Integrity always comes down to four specific actions:

- Welcoming all of your feelings, not hiding or denying anything you're feeling
- Telling the truth
- Keeping the agreements you have made (or consciously changing them with the other person)
- Taking 100 percent responsibility for any problem, activity, or life event in which you're involved. Less than 100 percent responsibility means you're operating as a victim. More than 100 percent means you're operating as a martyr.

If you and I are not doing these simple things, we don't feel good. That's really all there is to it. In other words, when we stonewall against our feelings, hide the truth, and ride roughshod over agreements we've made, we feel bad about ourselves. When we blame others or do the martyr's share of life's work, we feel bad about ourselves. Then we compound the problem by trying to feel better from the outside in. We buy things to feel better, we visit the plastic surgeon, we blame our discomfort on others. All because there is something inside us that is causing us to rattle and shimmy. When we do not feel good about ourselves, we need to train ourselves to look first for integrity breaches.

Integrity with Yourself

We cannot love ourselves if our actions are motivated by unexamined feelings. We cannot hold ourselves in high regard if there are truths we are hiding and agreements we have broken. The same energy that could be channeled into creative self-expression gets consumed by fixing the wobbles caused by a lack of integrity.

For example, I just heard a song on the radio written and sung by a person with whom I worked on songwriter's block. I've had the pleasure of working with a number of gifted artists on this and other artistic problems. I have nothing to offer them on the musical level. Instead, I help them unblock themselves by handling integrity breaches in their lives. Invariably, their blocks dissolve as they clear up their integrity issues. For one person the integrity breach is a failure to tell a guilty secret, such as an affair. For another it is denying a deep feeling or impulse—trying to keep something out of consciousness. For another artist it was trying to ignore the fact that he'd broken a number of agreements with key people in his life.

When they handled the integrity issue, whatever it was, their creativity flowed again. As one of my clients put it, "When I stopped lying to myself and other people, the music started again inside me."

If we are in integrity, we can think highly of ourselves. Integrity means being in equal partnership with other people and the universe itself. If we are out of integrity, we are pretending to be masters of the universe instead of in harmony with it. For example, if I break an agreement and blithely pretend it doesn't matter, I am separating myself from the universe. I am claiming that I am a special case, that I don't have to follow the rules of the game. This is asking for trouble, putting a Kick Me sign on my back that the universe can see.

Integrity with Others

Almost all problems in life can be overcome by being honest with ourselves and other people. My grandmother had a profoundly simple teaching on this subject. She said that if you told the truth all the time, you never had to remember what you said. She also said that if you did not tell the truth, it would throw everything in your system slightly out of kilter, and you would eventually "trip over your own shoelaces."

This story came to mind when I was invited on one of the talk shows during the scandal involving ice skater Tonya Harding. The show's host asked me to watch Harding's press conference on videotape and point out places where her body language suggested she was lying. It was not hard, because she was one of the worst and most obvious liars ever seen in public. For example, she almost always communicated in a tone of righteous indignation or whiny victimhood, two sure signs of the liar. After I showed the studio audience what to look for, they became quite skilled, and I set them to work spotting the body language of other truly awful liars from that spring's crop, including Michael Jackson and the Menendez brothers. My grandmother's theory even turned out to be uncannily accurate: Tonya had trouble with her shoelaces during the Olympics!

Before we move on, let me say again the most important thing I have learned about self-esteem: if I wake up some morning not feeling good about myself, I look for where I am out of integrity. I look for where I am not being honest with myself or someone else. I look for feelings I'm not letting myself feel, and I look for agreements I haven't kept. I fix these however I can—they usually take no more than a ten-minute phone call—and I almost always notice an immediate shift in my positive feelings toward myself.

Discovering Your Essence

Once you have checked out your integrity in the here-and-now reality of your life, you are ready to move on to a deeper level of learning to love yourself. Let's assume that you have handled the here-and-now issues that are compromising your integrity. Where do you look next for the key to your self-esteem?

Learn to separate your true self—your essence—from the changing and changeable phenomena of your life. Your feelings and your social masks come and go, but behind and beyond them is the vast space of essence. You learned, as I did, many personas in order to wend your way to where you are in your life. But beyond all our masks is the open space of essence, ready and waiting for us to tune in to it.

When you were a child, you learned a personality to get your needs met. In one family it worked to be quiet and helpful, perhaps, while another family responded to tantrums and whines. One family favored athletics, while another liked food. To survive and prosper in a family, you adopted the social masks that worked in that particular time and place.

If you grew up in a relatively healthy environment, you learned relatively healthy masks: Pleaser, Helper, Good Student. If your environment wasn't so healthy, you turned to more costly masks: Rebel, Clumsy Person, Problem Student.

The problem of successful people is that their "good" masks work really well. Strengths become weaknesses, especially at midlife. If your "persuasive" persona got you to the top of the legal profession, as one of my clients experienced, you may find, as he did, that it became his biggest obstacle in his after-forty quest to find his authentic self. A hundred times a day his "persuasive" voice kicked in to reassure him that all was okay, even though he actually felt like he was dying inside. A dozen times a week his "persuasive" persona convinced his wife that he really loved her, even though his actual physical body was having actual physical sex with his actual legal secretary. If he had believed his "persuader," as so many juries had, he was having the time of his life rather than rotting at the core.

As adulthood continues, it becomes necessary to remove all your masks in the search to answer the core question: who am I at my very core? It is easy to think that your positive masks are who you actually are. My lawyer client had been hearing feedback from his wife that his lawyer persona wasn't working very well at home. In fact, his attempts to argue persuasively with his wife and kids seemed to be the problem in his family. I suggested that he let go of the mask of needing to be right and proving other people wrong.

He shot me a withering look and said, "I make $350,000 a year with that mask. And you want me to give it up?"

"Not entirely," I replied. "Only when you are using it pro bono."

It is a challenge that successful people must someday face. We spend half our lives building up a set of masks that allow us to be successful in the world, only to find that genuine success in later life comes only through dismantling our carefully contrived personas. The real sweetness of life is attained only through communion with the authentic in ourselves. Nothing false ultimately brings satisfaction.

We need to take a close look at our social masks—the acts we put forward and the personas we adopt—because they play a major role in self-esteem. Personas are both our strength and our weakness. They not only enable us to survive childhood and succeed in adult life, they must be set aside later in life if we are to have an authentic experience of ourselves.

Early Imprints

Most of our masks grew out of the imprints we collected from people in our past. Certainly we need to slip free of the negative imprints, the limiting beliefs people had about us. But even if you received largely positive imprints, you still need to step clear of them. This is self-esteem we are talking about, not esteem in anyone else's eyes.

Our negative imprints affect how we handle every interaction of our lives: whether we tell the truth, whether we act responsibly, whether we allow ourselves to feel our feelings. As we will soon explore, these processes are central to healthy self-esteem.

We will never know where all of our negative imprints come from. All we can do is start from wherever we are and begin the process of finding any place we are operating from a limited view of ourselves. If you are honest with yourself, you won't have far to look.

Look carefully at the crucial imprint moments of your life, particularly your early life. Often in these moments we take on distorted and negative attitudes toward ourselves that come to light only later in life. These distorted imprints become the object of our focus. We fixate on them or try to pretend they don't exist. By fixing our attention on the imprint, we lose touch with the pure consciousness in which this imprint rests. The pure conscious—our essence—is always there, waiting for us to shift our attention to it.

Begin with conception, where our first loss of essence is likely to occur.

There are many ways you could have started your life. If you are lucky you may have been conceived consciously. Your parents may have thought carefully about creating a child and the eighteen-plus years of careful work that it would entail. They may have taken on this responsibility joyfully. They may have been secure enough in themselves to want to spend eighteen years carefully nurturing the essence of another human being. Or they may have been simply immersed in the sensual pleasure of sex and given no thought at all to your conception. They may have even been trying very hard not to conceive a child when you were conceived. Most studies indicate that the majority of us were unplanned and a substantial minority of us were actively unwanted. A shockingly high number of us were conceived in violence or under the influence of alcohol or other drugs.

To create a sound self-esteem, you need to take a careful inventory of any negative forces that were swirling around your conception. Many of our self-esteem problems don't actually have to do with us personally. For example, your parents may not have wanted a child when you were conceived, yet you were conceived by the biological forces present in the universe. Your parents may have sent negative energy at you from the moment of your conception. Often this negative energy is unconscious and continues in spite of their conscious efforts to pretend it isn't there. You need to look at these negative forces carefully so that you can separate out your self-esteem from the energy that was beamed at you from your earliest moments.

If you were unwanted, for example, that was really your parents' problem. It didn't have to do with you personally. They would have felt that way about anyone who happened to show up. Of course, it's easy to see how you could have taken it personally, but it didn't concern you at all. At that point they didn't think of you as a "you" but as an "it."

Knowing this fact will help you distinguish your own essence from the attitudes about you other people had. These negative attitudes get embodied—we carry them around inside us—and we sometimes allow those negative attitudes by others to contaminate our good feelings about ourselves.

Let's focus even more intently on the moment of your conception. As the sperm that would become you was being created in your father's body, feel what was going on in his life. You may have heard stories about what was going on with him, and you may not have. You may have stored memories in your cells that contain information, and you may not. No matter where you get the information, feel what was going on with your father. Did he have problems or concerns that could have given a negative flavor to your conception? Take any answers you get as hunches. The purpose of this inquiry is to celebrate your essence. As you wonder about these things, feel your own essence—who you really are—and distinguish your essence from your father's attitudes and energies. You actually are a completely separate being from your father, even though he contributed cells to your body.

Shift your wondering to your mother. As the egg that would become you was being prepared for your conception, feel what was going on in her life. Were there problems or concerns that could have created negative energy around your conception? Your mother already had her eggs when she was a fetus inside your grandmother, so part of you was inside your grandmother long ago.

Feel what was going on in your grandmother's life. Were there problems or concerns that could have created negative energy around your conception? Take whatever answers come as tentative hunches. The purpose of this inquiry is to celebrate your special essence, distinct from your mother and your father.

Tune in to the time you spent inside your mother, the prenatal time when you grew from a microscopic speck to the six or eight or ten pounds you weighed at birth. Were there issues or concerns going on around you, either in your mother's body or the world outside, that might have sent negative energy in your direction? For example, sometimes people feel ashamed about a baby's existence or try to hide it from the outside world. I have often found that the sense of shame many of my clients feel doesn't really even belong to them. It's someone else's shame that was laid upon them early in life when they were inside their mothers.

Take a moment now to feel your own essence, and distinguish it from the energies or attitudes directed toward you when you were inside your mother. Even if the energy was largely positive, you still need to separate out your good feelings about yourself from anyone else's feelings about you.

Let's focus on another early imprint moment: your first appearance out in the light. What was the reaction to you when you were born? Was there delight or drama or distaste? I saw one birth where the father unconsciously blurted out, "Oh no, it's a boy." He quickly tried to cover his outburst with an embarrassing series of disclaimers, but his spontaneous reaction was unforgettable. It makes me wonder how many of us got our welcome into the world contaminated with someone's negative energy toward us.

Feel whether disapproval was directed at you for any reason. Someone may have disapproved of you because of your very existence, or they may have disapproved of you because of some way you were an inconvenience to them. Just notice whether you feel that sense of disapproval—a feeling that you are wrong in some way—and feel it for a moment. With this feeling, as with any other feeling, it will lose its grip on you if you simply be with it for a few moments.

Attitudes are not the only thing that cloud our first experiences of life. Anesthesia, birth trauma, forceps, and illness are all common occurrences during birth. There is no agreement about the effects these things have on later life. All you can do is to be open to distinguishing your true essence from all the attitudes and uncontrollable events of your birth.

Begin right now. Take a moment to feel who you are, distinct from the occurrences of your birth.

The Persona Problem

As you grew, you adopted personas to survive in the family and place where you were born. Personas come in two flavors, adopted for two very different purposes. The first set of personas we adopt are largely benign and positive, because they are designed to get recognition from people around us. I call these your A personas, because they were usually adopted first in your life. Entertainers have their A material, the stuff they know works. I read an interview with Jerry Seinfeld in which he revealed his A joke, the one he always used when he felt he was losing a nightclub audience. I laughed out loud just reading it (and wish I could remember it so I could share it with you).

We all have our A personas, which worked early in our lives to get our needs met. An A persona is Cute Kid or Quiet Baby or Mom's Helper. One child may be Daddy's Girl, while another is the Class Clown. Your A personas are learned early on and added to later in life for the purpose of getting recognition from the world around you. In a state I once lived in, there was a politician who was earnest, fiscally responsible, likable, and conservative. I happened one day to meet his elementary school counselor from long ago. The counselor said that the boy's personas were identical to the man he would become later in life. As a youngster, he was always elected class treasurer because of his fiscal acumen, and he could be counted on as a playground monitor to keep the peace. He even wore a bow tie. As you can imagine, teachers loved him.

Our B personas are not so nice. They are adopted for a very different purpose. We usually resort to B personas when our A's fail to work. Faced with the pain of no recognition, we fall back on painful personas to get us through. B personas include Rebel, Sick Kid, Accident Prone, and Slow Learner.

The problems caused by these personas become especially evident in adult life. As we grow up, the need for these personas decreases. They were put in place to help us survive childhood; they are often not useful and even downright costly in adult life. There is a trend in adult life for your personas to separate from your essence; in adult life you increasingly wonder, "Who am I distinct from my programming?" This question begins to invite essence to come to the fore in your life. Then a battle begins between the forces of essence and the forces of persona in your life. Your essence wants enlightenment, your personas want survival. Most of us go back and forth many times before essence becomes a permanent backdrop of life.

The conservative politician I mentioned earlier had a classic problem with his A persona. At midlife, he unconsciously (I assume it was unconscious, anyway) set up a major crash of his A persona. He was caught in a scandal and forced to resign in public disgrace. Apparently the forces of his B personas were such that they could not be kept in check as he approached forty. There was a meltdown from which he has yet to recover. Yet, in a way, that is the best thing that could happen to us. At midlife it becomes crucial to reveal our essence, and if we do more of what worked earlier in our lives, we set ourselves up for many painful experiences as life tries to teach us to let go of even the personas that worked well.

One thing that causes our personas to remain glued in place is our tendency to defend ourselves when no defense is really required. A person may come up to you—perhaps a friend or family member—and say, "You are out of touch with your feelings." They are giving us feedback that our logical, reasonable persona is no longer serving us. How we respond to this feedback makes all the difference in the world.

Many of us keep our personas glued in place—long after they have ceased to serve us—by forming what I call "glue clubs."

These are networks of people whom we have enrolled in our personas. A true friend is a person who will help you get free of your personas, not keep them glued in place. But many of us do not have true friends, only members of a club that is designed to keep us the same.

Just how is the glue applied?

How We Keep Our Personas in Place

The glue is applied in four main ways. First, we glue our personas in place through justifying. We get some feedback from a friend or family member—"You are out of touch with your feelings"—and instead of using this information as an inspiration to inquire within, we justify why being out of touch with feelings is the correct approach to life.

Let me show you an example of defensiveness midway through a session with a corporate executive.

ME: Terry, I notice as you talk about your issues with the board of directors, your fists clench and unclench.

TERRY: Probably just a habit.

ME: Tune in and find out if there are some feelings there you need to be aware of.

TERRY: Nah.

ME: I notice you didn't take time to tune in; you just said "nah" right away.

TERRY: There you go again, focusing on things that probably don't have anything to do with anything.

Is he right? Am I just a picky guy with a fist fetish? Possibly, but listen to this first: Terry has flown across the country and is paying me thousands of dollars a day to help him deal with his anger problem. His outbursts are obviously costing him and the company enough that they are willing to make a fairly large investment in resolving them. Therefore, you would think that he would be more committed to solving the problem than to defending and justifying. But when the chips are down, we often retreat into our defenses, because they have helped us survive earlier in our lives. In Terry's case, his hostility kept his alcoholic and abusive father at bay. Even though his father is long buried, Terry doesn't know if he can survive without his rage.

A second way we keep our personas glued in place is to blame someone. Often we blame the very person who is trying to help us let go of our persona so essence can shine through. The act of blaming is an extreme form of being right, a habit that can be your most insidious hindrance in the quest for enlightenment. Many people, when given the opportunity to be happy and vibrant, settle instead for being right.

A third way of keeping your persona glued in place is to engage in a power struggle—to try to dominate others or to avoid their domination. While this power struggle is going on, life slips by with no creative participation on our part.

These three habits—justifying, being right, and playing power games—feed in to a fourth way of obscuring essence, which is through repeating old patterns. Each time we take an action, we strengthen the motivating force behind the action. For example, if you decide to quit smoking one day, you may feel the urge to smoke a hundred times before noon. Each time you feel the urge, you take ten deep breaths instead of smoking. So far, so good. However, at six in the evening, a friend stops by to say hello, and he is puffing on your favorite brand. You feel your biggest urge of the day, and it is powered by sheer desperation. You bum a smoke and suck it into your lungs. By waiting until you were desperate, you strengthened the feeling of desperation by rewarding it. Guess what signal your body will send you more quickly next time it wants a cigarette?

When we go on autopilot instead of creating a new response to life, our personas remain securely in place. There is safety in the familiar, and many of us wake up too late to the fact that a creative life does not run on trolley tracks but according to successive moments of choice.

Regardless of your personality, positive and negative aspects alike, it is not your essence. Essence is beyond personality. It's unlearned—a free gift of a lifetime—and it is everywhere at once in you. Your personality began to form at a particular time and place, but essence is timeless. Your personality shows up in specific actions, such as your speech, your habits, the way you smile, or the way you shake hands, but essence is always there in the background of all your positive and negative aspects.

Essence Is Felt

Essence is much easier to feel than it is to see or hear or touch. Personality can be easily seen in the way you walk or easily heard in the tone of your voice. Two people can speak the same word—*Taxi!*—and one says it with a sneer and a whine of entitlement while the other says it with presidential authority. These are their personalities made visible and audible. Take a moment now to go beneath and beyond your personality, to feel your essence distinct from your personality. Let yourself know that your essence—your true identity—does not depend on anything you ever learned.

As you grew up, you also developed feelings, thoughts, and moods. You learned to be scared in certain situations, angry in others, sad in others. Your moods would be up and down, depending on many factors. You could get in a low mood by missing some sleep or overdoing it with sweets. Your feelings could run wild if you were exhausted. Take a moment now to distinguish your essence from all your feelings, your thoughts, and your mood. All those things may change, but in the background there is always that vast open sky of essence against which all the changing phenomena in your body and mind play out.

Self-esteem means prizing and valuing the person you truly are. Integrity takes the wobble out of your existence so that you can feel and sense your true self free from constant uproar. Distinguishing your essence from your personas allows you to focus on the peripherals and ephemerals of social masks. Ultimately, loving yourself takes you beyond acceptance, prizing, and valuing to a realm in which your essence is absolutely equal and seamlessly connected to the essence of others and the universe.

CHAPTER 6

Building on Self-Esteem

How to Find Peace of Mind, Body, and Heart

To find genuine self-esteem, you need to know how to create peace in your mind, your body, and your heart. You need to know methods open to everyone, methods that exclude no one and have no side effects. For example, some people claim to have found peace through methods that exclude people, perhaps by taking psychedelic drugs or becoming a born-again member of a religious group. Others have found peace through sitting in isolation tanks or developing a relationship with a guru. There is nothing fundamentally wrong with these methods, but they all exclude someone and many have side effects. Some people are allergic to LSD, while others are allergic to fundamentalism or incense.

The path I'm describing is open to all. The organic methods of conscious living are free—they are our natural birthright—and they are completely free of side effects. You can use the techniques whether you are Buddhist or Christian or Jew. They go beneath the surface to deal with the source of the turmoil in human beings. The techniques show us how to quiet the turmoil regardless of what has caused it.

Self-Esteem and the Art of Handling Fear

Most of us, especially if we grew up around brothers or sisters, have to overcome several main fears from childhood. These fears come up later in life even in the lives of very successful people. In fact, the more success you have in life, the more likely you are to flush up these fears. To release our full potential and develop self-esteem, we need to look at our fears.

Each time you go through a big transition in your life—such as having a baby or publishing a book or opening a restaurant—you break through into the unknown. You are outside your normal box, especially if the transition involves some creative expansion on your part. When these expansions happen, self-esteem issues—particularly the fears I will describe—come to the surface. Part of you wants to break through into the unknown, into a higher and finer version of yourself. But part of you wants to stay in the comfort zone, the zone of the known. If this part of you were on a car, it would be called the governor. A governor is a gadget that automatically keeps you from going too fast. When you get to its predetermined limit, it does something to your engine that slows it down.

Most of us come equipped with the psychological version of such a gadget. The Governor wants to keep you safe, because you have survived in your limited box, if not thrived there. The Governor is not convinced you can live in the rarefied air of the new space you have created. It may even conspire to sabotage your project so you will not have to develop the skills necessary to operate at a higher level. The Governor's tool is usually one of the following fears.

The Central Fear of People with Low Self-Esteem

There is one major fear that you and I must handle to live in good self-esteem: thinking we are fundamentally flawed in some way. When we are in thrall to this fear, we think thoughts like:

- What's wrong with me?
- What's wrong with them?
- What did I do to deserve this?
- Why can't things ever go right for me?

When we are in thrall to this fear, we tune in to our bodies and feel:

- An emptiness deep inside
- A sense of despair
- A conviction that life will never turn out right

Many of us suffer from this fear, and it keeps us locked forever in the zone of the known.

When things do not go smoothly—when we encounter adversity—many of us go immediately into three dead-end questions:

What is wrong with me? What is wrong with them? What is wrong with the world? All three of these questions are based on the central fear that we are fundamentally flawed in some way. Once you shake this fear off, you are free to ask a more fruitful question: What needs to be done here to meet my chosen goals? This is a question a scared person or a person with low self-esteem cannot ask.

In a lifetime of doing therapy, I've seen the fear of being fundamentally flawed arise out of hundreds of different life moments. Sometimes it comes from conception, if we are conceived in a fundamentally unloving way. Sometimes it comes later in life, when our feelings are developing. Many of us grew up in families where we were singled out for shame if we felt scared or sad or sexual. Even later, in school, there are many potential moments when we can conclude that there is something fundamentally wrong with us, especially the way our particular brain operates.

My wife, Kathlyn, has to be moving in order to learn. If you watch her writing or even reading a book, her toes are wiggling or some other part of her body is in constant motion. She did poorly in school for the first three years, because her teachers tried to get her to sit still. Finally, she had the great good fortune to come into the classroom of Mrs. Morgan, an inspired teacher who had a different way of solving the problem. She let Kathlyn sit at the end of the row, where she had more space around her. She also encouraged her to move as much as she wanted. Overnight Kathlyn became the gifted learner she always was and always would be. She made straight A's right on through to her Ph.D.

I wish all of us could have our own Mrs. Morgan sometime in our lives. Because we do not, however, many of us come into adult life with a sense that there is something wrong with us. This is the central fear.

Handling Fear

What can we do about it? Fear is a different emotion from anger or sadness. You can pound out your anger and sob out your sadness. Fear, though, does not have an explosive cathartic movement that discharges it from our bodies. With fear, you use a different strategy.

The First Move to Handle Fear: When you are feeling fear, first you acknowledge that it's there by placing your nonjudgmental attention on it. Like shining your flashlight on the monster in your darkened bedroom when you were a kid, putting the light of attention on fear makes it show up for what it is. Fear really is only a vibration down in the middle of your body, accompanied by a racy, slightly queasy sensation.

The Second Move to Handle Fear: When you are feeling fear, breathe in the direction of the sensations. Nature has wired us with a sensitive breathing apparatus, which causes us to restrict our breathing when we're scared. Take a few deep, slow breaths, and your fear will begin to dissolve.

These two moves come together in one simple flow: you feel the fear in your body and breathe to embrace it. It's like you might greet a friend: you nod hello and then give him or her a hug. When we greet fear with a hello and embrace, it disappears. The psychiatrist Fritz Perls said, "Fear is excitement without the breath." You can prove this remarkable observation to yourself. Breathe down through the middle of any anxiety you feel, now or later. Within a few deep, slow breaths, it usually begins to melt into a pleasant sensation of heightened attention.

Now that you have greeted your new friend and embraced it with a hug, you are ready to dance.

The Third Move to Handle Fear: Move your body to accommodate your fear.

Some of us, like Kathlyn, are mover-learners. If you are one of those, shift your body around when you are feeling scared, and the fear will begin to dissolve. Take a few breaths, and change your body position consciously. It makes a world of difference.

As you dance, you can carry on a conversation about fear, which is the next move.

The Fourth Move to Handle Fear: Communicate about fear straightforwardly.

Fear dissolves when we communicate about it in the same tone of voice we use to tell the time of day. "It's ten-thirty and I'm afraid" is the attitude to take toward communicating fear. If you make fear no big deal, it becomes no big deal.

All these moves, while powerfully useful, are preparations for the ultimate way to handle fear and every other moment of life.

The Ultimate Move to Handle Fear: The ultimate healing move is to love your fear unconditionally. Fear is an implosion, a rushing of energy toward the center of you in a movement of contraction. When you love your fear, you embrace it in a field of warmhearted, open space. When you love your fear, you give it room to breathe, and this is often all it needs.

You may need to love your fear a thousand and one times before the cure becomes permanent. The reason is that you may awaken the fear each time you expand to a new version of your self. Each time you step through the gate into the unknown, you may encounter the dragon. The dragon is really the limiting part of yourself, trying to keep you imprisoned in the zone of the known, where you are safe.

Our fears are often so big that love is the only thing that can contain them. Love is the ultimate healer because it can contain its opposite: you can love yourself for hating yourself. Sometimes our fear, and our self-hate, is so great that all we can do is love it. I have watched, deeply moved, as many people have discovered the power of love in therapy. I have seen people love their anger, their fear, the wrongdoings of the past, and the transgressions of others against them. I have seen love smooth out the roughest of vibrations that shake the human organism.

There is no test I've ever seen love fail.

Now that we have looked into the central fear that lives within us to cloud our sense of self-esteem, let's move to the next.

The Second Fear That Limits Self-Esteem

The second fear that limits self-esteem is the fear of outdoing others and leaving them behind. This fear is deeply rooted in our minds and bodies. Many people—particularly gifted people—hold themselves back from reaching their full potential because to do so would be to outshine someone, and that someone is usually from long ago in the past. We fear the loss and loneliness of abandoning people in our past, even though we feel a deep calling to pursue our own destinies.

Australian therapists have a colorful name for the "outdoing" problem, based on one of their cultural motifs. They call it the "tall poppy syndrome." If a poppy stands out too tall above the other poppies, the farmer will cut it off. Australian parents admonish their children not to be "tall poppies." Stay with the pack, don't attract attention to yourself, don't make others look bad. Otherwise you'll pay the price.

Part of the culture of Australia comes out of the jailhouse consciousness of convicts who were sent there in chains. In prisons, there is understandable emphasis on not sticking too far out of the crowd. "Keep your head down in the pack" is the prevailing ethic, lest a prison guard take a fancy to using his stick on you (or take a fancy to you, period).

This syndrome crimps self-esteem, and the more you succeed the worse it gets. Many gifted people find that they cannot enjoy their success because of the gnawing guilt of having outdone others, of having left others behind. One of my first therapy clients after I got my Ph.D. was an enormously talented woman who was also prodigiously miserable. As we explored why this was so, we uncovered numerous layers of the fear we are discussing. She was a prodigy as a child, and her sister was not. She grew up in constant fear of outshining her sister, and the more accolades she received on the concert stages of the East Coast, the worse the guilt became. Finally, psychosomatic problems caused her to abandon music. This was her unconscious solution to making the fear go away.

As we worked through this layer, her symptoms began to disappear, but then we came to an even more deeply ingrained issue. She was one of the very few survivors of a family that had perished in the Holocaust. How could she value her life, appreciate her beauty, and enjoy the success she earned when every breath she took meant she was outdoing and outliving her relatives? That was a question that took months of careful work on her part to answer.

Whom are you outdoing with the successes of your life? That is your question to answer, and mine, too. Just now, in writing about this question, I burst into sobs remembering my beloved Aunt Catherine. Kat, as I called her, was a Down's syndrome baby born into a family of three brilliant older sisters. My grandparents were trying, too late in life, to have the son they would never have. Kat was an eternal child with perpetually sunny disposition. She was my constant companion growing up. Even though she was much older than I, she was my number one playmate up until the time I went to school. One of the saddest moments of my young life was seeing the grief-stricken look on Kat's face as I walked off to school for the first time. She was being left behind again.

Later in life, as I began to work on my self-esteem, I realized I was carrying a fear of outshining Kat. I loved her deeply, and I did not want her to hurt. I could see that it hurt her to watch me being able to do things, like reading and writing, that she could not do. I began to avoid her subtly after I entered grade school because I felt that I had to dampen myself around her.

I wish we had spoken openly about it. I wish I could have said, "I'm sorry that I'm leaving. I'm going to miss you, but I have to fulfill my own destiny. Let me hug you while we both cry." That conversation was more than my six-year-old mind could muster.

I see now that this issue is one of the dominant themes of my life, and perhaps it is of yours. Ethologists tell us that 5 to 10 percent of herds tend to roam off by themselves, and for better or for worse, I seem to be in that small band of wanderers. I must move on; there is someplace I feel I must go to fulfill my dreams, and there are people I must leave behind in order to do it. I always move on, but in the past I have often done it in a way that leaves emotional debris behind. Sometimes it has seemed like leaving was tinged with desperation, a matter of life and death for me. I do not communicate about it consciously until much later. Then I go back, if I can, to make the bridge again.

The Third Limiting Fear

Self-esteem is compromised by a third fear. We were a burden to someone long ago, and this sense of our burdensomeness pervades our lives today. As we go through life we feel that we do not deserve to take up space. Who are we to dare to dream? We interfered with someone's dreams long ago, and we are convinced it was our fault.

This is a hard one for me to write about, because it played such a painful role in my own life. In one sense, my very existence ruined my mother's life. I became the burden she had to bear and the daily reminder of the fickleness of life. I wrote in the introduction to the book about my father's sudden death and its consequences for my mother.

I don't remember ever seeing a smile on my mother's face. I have gone through every family photo, looking for the smile I never saw, and there are plenty of pictures with smiles before I was born. She is beaming at her wedding, and she is beaming at my brother in many photos my father must have taken. Because of the changed circumstances, there are few pictures of me. In the one baby picture of me and my mother, she looks down at me as if I were a ball and chain. My wife calls it "the photo that launched a thousand therapy sessions," because it expresses such a deep sense of anguish and burden.

Fortunately for us both, my mother was an incredibly strong person. She also had my grandmother living up the street, and as a wise therapist once told me, "One good grandmother is worth two pediatricians and a carload of shrinks." I was put into good hands, but the deep sense of unwantedness stayed down in my cells for many years.

Were you a burden in your early life? This is a question you and I should think about, because it has such a profound effect on our self-esteem. No matter how far you go, you may find the lingering sense of burden holding you down, holding you back. I have worked with many highly successful people who still struggled with this fear.

A famous writer sits in my office, discussing his writer's block. It is our first session. He asks, "Does the world really need another book? Why should I waste another acre of the Canadian forest, making paper for a book that will just sit on people's shelves after they read it? What's the point?" I pause to digest this, then I ask,

"Were you a burden to your family when you were little?" His face falls, "Yes, in a huge way. Why do you ask that?"

I explain to him how the fear of being a burden works. He tells me a deeply wrenching story of hard times and loss. He was the scapegoat of his alcoholic father's rage, another mouth to feed in an already overcrowded house. He was the straw that broke the camel's back. He defined himself by escaping his hardscrabble life, and he made his fortune telling stories about it, but now in his middle years he cannot escape the feeling that he is a burden, that he does not deserve "to breathe the air of this fine planet," in his poetic phrase. We talk for an hour about the problems of feeling that you are a burden, and at the end of the session I casually ask him to take notes on what we have discussed. I take mine as he takes his. He finishes first, and I see tears in his eyes as he hands me his page. "This is the first thing I've written in a month," he says. "The fog is beginning to lift."

I am happy but not really surprised. My own fog lifted each time I confronted one of these major fears in myself. Life conspires with us to bring all our fears up into our face. If we look at them and welcome them into the wholeness of ourselves, symptoms simply disappear.

The Fourth Limiting Fear

Many of us do not grow in our self-esteem because to rise to a higher potential would mean disloyalty to our family or our clan. Often there is one person in our background to whom we must remain loyal, even though that person may have terrible problems and may have caused us enormous suffering. This fear differs slightly from outdoing. The later involves going beyond another person's achievement. Loyalty involves clinging to a bond formed earlier in life.

Are there people in your past to whom you are bound by hidden loyalties? We need to ask ourselves: have we sealed a deal with someone to remain at a lower level of self-esteem or success or love than we might be capable? I know I made such a deal with my father, even though I never knew him in real life. Somehow—I still don't know how—I made an unconscious pact with him to carry on his script of obesity and addiction. It took me into my twenties to spot the deal and break the spell. When I woke up, I saw how ironic it all was. My brother, who had known my father for seven years, had none of the problems that plagued my father's life. My brother did not smoke and was not obese. I, who had never known my father in the flesh, was carrying out his tradition to the letter in my own flesh. Even though I have been a psychologist half my life, I still shake my head over how that can be.

Our unconscious belief is: "If I break out of the trance into a higher level of self-esteem, I will show that I am disloyal and something bad will happen to me or to them." The trance requires that we not rock the boat by being more successful or thinking more highly of ourselves than the person to whom we are loyal.

Expressing Our Creative Potential

We come now to the issue of creative expression in our lives, and here the rule is simple. If you are expressing your creative potential, you get to feel good about yourself. If you are not, you don't. I consider this the ultimate issue we need to resolve with regard to our self-esteem. After we have come to love ourselves unconditionally, after we have handled our integrity issues, after we have sorted out our essence from our personas, and after we have learned to handle our fears, we are faced with bringing forth the fullness of ourselves. In many ways, this is the ultimate challenge.

There are dreams that live in our hearts and souls. We are called to birth them, nurture them, and bring them to fulfillment. There are awesome barriers to accomplishing this task, no matter whether your dream is writing the ultimate novel or cooking a transcendent clam chowder. The barriers are in ourselves, in society, and in just about any other place you might care to look. In many ways, crossing all the barriers to your creative expression is what life is all about.

If Thomas is not to be doubted, Jesus addressed this problem squarely. It appears in one of the most powerful passages in the scriptures (perhaps so powerful that it was kept out of the final version of the Bible). In the Gospel of Thomas, Jesus says, "If you bring forth what is within you, what is within you will save you. If you do not bring forth what is within you, what is within you will destroy you." It's easy to see why this passage got deleted from the official canon. It is not a message you would want falling into the hands of the general public if your goal was to control them. People reading this would be inspired to look within themselves for the source of creativity, not outside toward the authorities. Truth would be spoken even in places where it was inconvenient. Everyone would want to be a prophet and a poet; the worker-bee population would decline precipitously.

I have noticed that people who are working to express their creativity feel good about themselves whether they are rich or poor. I have a client worth tens of millions of dollars who was foundering in her life. Then she transformed herself by making a heartfelt commitment to her creativity. Now she gets out of bed each morning and writes for two hours before her kids get up. She has not published any of her writings and has no intention to. It's just for her.

That's an important distinction, and one that I have had to face many times in my career. I started writing for the pure pleasure of it; I love the act of creation, of seeing ideas appear on the page where none have been before. I love the challenge of finding a voice in which to express the ideas, the joy of getting the right metaphor or example to illustrate what I'm expressing. I got published almost as soon as I started writing, though, and then an unexpected new set of problems opened up. The original poems had leaped out of me joyfully, like dolphins jumping for the sake of play. I offered a workshop on poetry in counseling at the annual convention, and it was standing-room only. Spotting a hot trend, the journal wanted more poems in a hurry, and I sat down to write them "to order." They didn't come easily at all—more like dolphins on Valium—because now I had a goal and a set of expectations. I was writing for an audience, which, although tiny, made a difference in how I expressed myself. I lost the ability to write poetry purely for myself, purely for play, and soon I lost interest in writing poems altogether. Later I found a way to get my poet-self back, but at the time I simply felt like the well had run dry and I didn't know why.

Creativity also plays a key role in relationships. When I work with a couple, I listen to the content of their problem as they describe it. With my third ear, though, I am listening for the creativity issue behind the problem. Many couples create drama in their lives because they are not facing some creative issue. They may want to create a business or a dream house or a baby together, and because they are unwilling to face some aspect of this creation, they spin their wheels in the mud of some problem instead.

I see this problem played out also in the lives of people with addiction problems. Many of the substance abuse clients I've worked with are incredibly creative people. Their minds are abuzz with creative ideas all day long, so much so that they often use the substance to quiet things down, to turn down the volume on their creativity for a while. Often, too, they do not handle success very well; they don't think they deserve it, so they often mess up before, during, or right after a big worldly success.

The Overflow Issue

I had to face another problem when I began to express my creativity. Once I turned the tap on, I found I had many more creative ideas than I could possibly act on, and I had to figure out what to do with the overflow. I think this issue may be true of creative people in general. Successful ones just learn how to handle it better than their foundering colleagues. Some people do not think they are creative at all. In other words, they don't turn the tap on. This is pure learned bunk, however, since almost all of us have genius-level potential in some area or another. Once they get the tap on, though, they have the what-to-do-with-the-overflow problem. Some people try to drown out their excess creative ideas through food, drink, and distractions. Others try to act on them all, and they drive themselves to distraction.

That was my tendency. I would try to do too much and would end up feeling frazzled. Things would fall through the cracks. It has taken a great deal of pride swallowing and discipline to acknowledge that I can accomplish only a couple of big projects and a few more small projects in the course of a year. The trick is to let all your ideas pour through and celebrate them as the gift of a creative life. Carefully select those that have the deepest heart connection for you and that will make the biggest difference in the world. That's the way I've learned to do it, anyway.

I have also found that it helps to do some creative work every day, even if I don't have a major project going on. I think of it as keeping the pipes oiled. If I have time, I like to act on some of the fringe projects my mind comes up with. In the past couple of years I have written several feature-length screenplays as well as outlines for a couple of others. I have also written two children's books and a host of shorter pieces. These have been primarily for my own amusement—to keep the flow going—and so that I could learn other forms of writing.

Years ago, an acquaintance of mine had lunch with Picasso. Throughout a two-hour lunch, Picasso's hands were never idle; he doodled, sketched, and drew, going through dozens of napkins, many of which he gave away to lucky diners. He even did a pencil sketch on the wood of the table. I think of this as a model for how to nourish our creativity. Keep it flowing, don't worry about the outcome, then put some serious focus into a few projects that you want to make a difference with.

Deathbed Goals

Many years ago I got the gift of a great question from a friend, Ed Steinbrecher. He asked me, "What are the four or five top goals for your life?" He was asking me to step forward into the future, into the successful completion of my life, and ask myself, "What did you accomplish or experience that made your life a success?" It's a great question, and I'm grateful to Ed for bringing it up to me just when I most needed it. I have since asked thousands of people that same question, always with fruitful results.

I realized there were just a few things that were crucial to me and that I would not feel complete unless I had done everything within my power to make them happen. They had always been in the deep background of my awareness, but I had not brought them front and center. They were:

- To create a harmonious long-term relationship with a woman—a union in which both of us could express our full potential
- To live in a state of completion (nothing important unspoken or undone) with my family and close friends
- To generate a complete written record of everything of value I have learned and put it in a form that I could pass down to succeeding generations
- To savor and enjoy all the moments of my life
- To get as complete as possible an understanding of and resonance with the laws of the universe and its creator force

Once I got clear on my "deathbed" goals, I felt an even greater sense of peace and well-being come over me. Now I knew what I was about. They were all things that rested on my own efforts; they required no one else to change. I could tell at any given moment whether I was moving in their direction or doing something that was extraneous to my chosen goals. Best of all, they inspired me to get moving on them. There was no law that said I had to wait for my deathbed to manifest these goals. Once I had my attention on them, it only took me a short time to manifest them (although they are ongoing and need daily attention). I cannot describe the sense of peace I have gained from figuring out my priorities.

As we saw in chapter 3, one of the required lessons for learning was to let go of the uncontrollable. Your deathbed goals should consist only of those things that are completely within your control. Don't set as a goal something like "To be loved by a beautiful woman/man." Whether someone loves you is not within your control. Instead, set as a goal, as I did, something that is within your control: to create a harmonious relationship with a woman in which I can fully express my relationship potential.

I have not found it easy—in myself or in my clients—to distinguish between the deepest goals and those that are merely transitory. After many years of experimentation, I discovered a way that has proven very useful. To find out if a goal is what you really want, step into an imaginary future, and imagine yourself looking back to where you are right now. From the future perspective, ask yourself, "Is this what I really wished I had done?" One of my clients had the problem of trying to decide whether to go to medical school or to spend time traveling in Asia. When she used the imaginary future technique, she discovered that she really wanted to jump right into medical school, which she had been resisting because of pressures from her family, which were getting in the way of listening to her own heart. Once she tuned in, the answer was right there in a matter of seconds.

Self-Esteem Depends on Emotional Literacy

From moment to moment, our bodies flicker and flow with feelings. If we don't know ourselves on an emotional level, we don't know ourselves at all. I have spent over half my life in the hot world of human emotion. By now I have probably seen every form of every emotion, from the tiny teardrops of a socialite's polite sob to the awesome rage of a psychotic patient who required me and six burly attendants to restrain him. From that perspective, I would have to say that emotional literacy is more important than the more familiar kind of cognitive literacy. No one ever went to prison because of bad grammar, but the prisons are full of people who are there because of emotional illiteracy. I am pleased that many schools have begun including material on emotion and communication in the curriculum, although much more needs to be done. I would like to share with you the most precious learnings

I've gleaned about how to handle emotions. Most of these learnings have come the proverbial hard way, through making a thousand and one painful mistakes that I later chose to call "learning opportunities." Others came through making suggestions to therapy clients and watching the results happen in their lives.

From all this I've learned: peace of heart is as important as peace of mind. There are things we all need to know about our feelings, and I will begin with the most important lesson in the curriculum of emotional literacy:

1. Start noticing your body sensations, and use them just as you use your other senses. Your body sensations are the eyes and ears of your inner world; they will give you crucial information you need for running your life. The neurologist David Hubbard says, "If you ignore your body sensations, you are exactly in the same position as you would be driving your car down the freeway with your eyes shut and your ears plugged. You might make it a mile or two, but it would be sheer luck." Your body sensations are an exquisitely tuned signal system honed over millions of years of evolution. Your sensations speak their own language and must be listened to carefully if you wish to understand them.

Here are two examples. You are watching a television show, and you notice your stomach muscles are clenching. You tune in to this sensation and realize that the subject of the television show is reminding you of something you are dealing with in your own life. The show is about children getting into trouble, and you realize you need to talk to your child about an issue that concerns you. Your inner feedback system of your body sensations has given you a cue about an action you need to take.

You are about to leave work to pick up your kids from day care just as your boss comes rushing in with something that needs to be done right away. You notice a slight headache begin in the back of your neck, and you realize you are angry. You say, "That doesn't seem fair," and the headache lessens. He says, "I'm sorry, you're right. It can wait until tomorrow." Your inner signal system has guided you again to take effective action.

A great deal depends on our ability to listen to the inner symphony of our sensations. If we don't, we are driving down the road with our inner eyes shut. Potential disaster lies ahead. If you become skilled at noticing your sensations, you have an extra sense you can use throughout the day. Sensations are also the gateway to your feelings. Indeed, feelings are simply sensations that occur reliably enough to have names attached to them.

Before we can name our feelings, we have to attend to the fields of information swirling inside us all day long.

Now for the second lesson in the curriculum of emotional literacy:

2. Learn to name the common feelings and locate them in your body. Until I learned to name my feelings, they often felt bigger than I was. When I got so I knew the difference between anger and fear and sadness, and could locate them in my body, I realized I was bigger than they were. Most feelings don't need much more than a passing nod. They are just passing through, but you are going to be around a long time.

The most important ones to name are:

I'm scared . . .
I'm angry . . .
I'm sad . . .
I'm longing for . . .
I'm excited . . .
I'm happy . . .
I'm sexually attracted . . .
I love . . .

My life went more smoothly as I learned to say those feeling statements, especially to the significant people in my life. It was crucial to learn to say them with Kathlyn and my children, but I also made a great deal of progress saying them in other situations, as well. For example, I had a number of unpleasant interactions with a dean of the university where I taught for twenty years. I would often come away from meetings with him feeling angry and humiliated. Applying some of the medicine I mentioned above, I discovered there was hurt beneath my anger. Finally I got up the courage to tell him how hurt I felt when he interrupted me and others and how afraid I felt when he would turn red and pound on his desk.

The problem shifted just by telling him the truth. Halfway through the conversation I realized he was another one of those male authority figures on whom I was projecting my father. I was a storm of hurt and anger waiting to blow. I told him about all this, and even though he was a loudly proclaimed foe of psychology, he listened with a rapt expression on his face. The proof of the pudding came later: he never interrupted me or pounded on the desk again, and I never saw him do it with others.

Finding Your Feelings in Your Body

A key part of the process is learning where you feel your feelings. Making a body map of your feelings can be very helpful. I have done it many times over the years, and each time I have noticed more and more useful detail about my emotions.

I feel fear down in the middle of my body, around and behind my navel. Fear spreads its antsy icicles up into my chest, and sometimes, if I'm really scared, I feel a clutchy sensation in my throat. Sadness feels very different to me. I feel it as a pressure in my chest and a lumpy feeling in my throat. I can feel a tugging at my eyes, along with a slight moistening, even if I am not going to cry.

Anger was the hardest feeling for me to get in touch with. With a few decades' perspective, I can now see why it was so difficult for me. It occurs for me as a tightening of my arms, shoulders, and back of the neck. I also feel it in my jaw. These areas had always been so tight that it was hard to notice much difference when I was angry. I had been angry so long I didn't know there was any other way to be. After a few sessions of simple relaxation exercises, I let go of some of the tension in my body and became able to feel more sensation. Then I could feel anger come and go. As I became more sensitive, I noticed that it flickered on and off dozens of times a day, usually in response to trivial situations where life wasn't going according to my expectations.

Excitement is an all-over feeling for me. When I'm excited, I feel a slight tingle that is hard to localize. It's definitely a more subtle feeling than sexual arousal and much less localized than fear or sadness. I wonder if the feeling of excitement may affect the primitive capillary bed, a system of potential sensation throughout the body that if laid out in a line would run sixty thousand miles long. The capillary bed spreads over almost the entire body and may account for the all-over aspect of excitement.

I get a similar all-over sensation when I'm happy. Happiness also comes with a light warmth from my chest, a pleasant champagne bubble sensation of a large number of tiny things in movement. Kathlyn and I often say "I'm happy" to each other around the house; it is probably our most frequent emotional communication to each other. This has led to some funny moments out in the world. One day I was working out on an exercise bike at the gym, lined up in a row with a dozen or so puffing grown-ups, none of whom I knew. Forgetting where I was, I burst out with "I'm happy!" which earned me a large number of quickly swiveled heads and wary glances.

When I tune in to sexual arousal, I feel it not only in my genitals but also from deep in my lower abdomen. It is a pleasant, streaming sensation that can come and go many times during the course of a day. With this sensation, I do not make a practice of stating it every time I feel it.

And now for the third lesson:

3. Say something authentic about your feelings when you feel them, if you want to feel intimate with the person you're talking to. Say your feeling to the person who triggered it, but be willing to learn that it goes far beyond that person. Human beings are much more sensitive than we give ourselves credit for. We feel hurt often, and we often do things that cause others to feel hurt. If you speak up when you feel hurt, you will learn something very important. Often you'll find that the hurt was based on misunderstanding, not on anyone's conscious attempt to hurt you. But you don't get to find that out if you don't say anything about it. Swallowed hurts are the fuel for a host of ills, most of which can be prevented if we are honest and forthright about speaking up.

One of the important learnings of life is: you're seldom upset for the reason you think you are. Your headache may have been triggered by your boss, and telling him is an important place to start. But don't stop there. Always ask yourself, "What does this remind me of?" and "Is this familiar?" Many things that trigger us during the course of a day are replays of old dramas, often beginning in our families. Your original headache may have been a response to your demanding father, and your demanding boss is simply a replica of a series of authoritarian people you've entertained in your life.

Speak the truth of fear and anger as well as hurt. We need to get in the habit of saying, "I felt afraid when you said . . ." and "I was angry when ______ happened." By speaking the truth of our feelings, we let people know us better. We also keep from building up a load of unexpressed feelings that have to be dumped later or buried deeper.

Hurt is a good one to start with, because it is at the bottom of a lot of the anger people feel toward one another. Next time you feel angry, check beneath it and I predict you'll find, as I often have, that you felt hurt before you got angry. Learning to say "I felt hurt when . . ." probably deserves to be the first lesson of the curriculum for emotional literacy, whether you learn it in the first grade, as a senior in college, or as a senior citizen.

4. Get skilled at spotting the signs of feelings in other people, and pay attention to them when they occur. Say something about these signs to people you want to be closer to, and invite them to notice them in you. We cause ourselves a great deal of trouble by overlooking and overriding other people's feelings. They are just as sensitive as we are and are constantly exhibiting the signs of feelings going on inside them. With commitment and practice, you can read the signs. You will transform your relationships in the wink of an eye.

Take notice when you see the flicker of irritation cross a friend's face. Pause and say, "I just saw what looked like a flicker of irritation cross your face. What's happening?" Sometimes you'll make contact, other times you'll get back a flurry of defensiveness. It doesn't really matter. I can guarantee you that you don't want friends who get defensive when you point out such things. Take notice when a clenched jaw catches your awareness. Say "I notice your jaw is clenched" to the person. If he or she reflects on your observation and tells you the truth about what's going on, keep that person in your friendship circle.

One of the reasons "polite" society makes so many people sick is that we have been brainwashed to overlook the obvious signs of feelings, to pretend they are not there. We are not supposed to notice the sweat pouring down Richard Nixon's face as he reassures us he's not a crook. We are supposed to avert our eyes from the obvious so as not to rock the boat.

According to historians, all this overlooking of the obvious grows out of our religious heritage. At a certain point in the Middle Ages it became acceptable to lie if the purpose of the lie was to protect the authority of the church. Once this way of thinking became established, it began to be applied to many situations, with terrible results that deeply affect society today:

- It's all right to lie to protect Dad so that we can keep the status quo in the family.
- One of O. J. Simpson's friends said that it was all right to lie to protect O. J., because black people have been the subjects of racial injustice.
- It's all right to lie to the common folk, because telling them the truth would get them upset.
- It's all right to lie to protect myself, because telling the truth would have an unsettling effect on people around me.
- It's all right to lie to your spouse about the affair you're having, because to tell the truth would be just plain cruel. (I actually heard this one proclaimed by a famous person on a talk show recently. The audience clapped vigorously.)

And so it goes, to the point where we are now virtually oblivious to most of the obvious signs of feelings going on in ourselves and other people. We look the other way, and our national health costs keep going up and up.

What is the alternative? It is very simple, but be prepared to put in a lot of practice time until it becomes second nature. To make the following move goes against virtually everything you have been taught about how to function in polite society.

YOU: How are you, John?

JOHN: Fine. (As he says this his eyes dip down and he rubs his forehead.)

YOU: I notice as you said "Fine" your eyes dipped down and you rubbed your forehead.

Don't do this unless you want to have a more intimate relationship with John. If you are content to skate superficially through your relationship with John, overlook the signs of feeling. But if you want to be closer, if you value him as a friend, notice the obvious.

JOHN: (reeling from shock) Uh, yeah. I'm actually terrible. My wife just told me this morning she's moving in with her therapist.

YOU: I'm sorry to hear that. Is there any way I can help?

Such moments are the richness of life. Don't miss out on them. I missed out on them for half my life. I grew up in a family where we were actually punished for noticing the obvious. So I retreated behind a wall of oblivion. The wall didn't stop the world from occurring, it just stopped me from participating in it. Fortunately, I woke up in time. Now my life is rich with many feeling moments. My wife and I have an agreement that we want to have our feeling signs observed and fed back to each other.

KATHLYN: I noticed when you were on the phone your voice seemed tight and constricted.

GAY: (pauses to reflect) Thanks. I realize I was agreeing to do something I don't really want to do.

I can't guarantee you it goes that smoothly every time, though. Sometimes we won't welcome the message, especially if one of us is tired or harried or caught up in some resistance.

KATHLYN: I noticed when you were on the phone . . .
GAY: Oh, I'm in a hurry right now. I don't have time for that!

Then we have to sit down and renew our commitment to knowing the truth, seeing the truth, speaking the truth. Sometimes our urge to return to oblivion is stronger than our urge toward enlightenment. I predict yours will be, too, on occasion. That's why I don't hold myself to perfection. There will be lots of slips along the way, and the best I can do for now is to use the slips as opportunities to make a stronger commitment. I keep my eye on the frequency of such slips of commitment. If they are happening less often than they were a year ago, I feel as if I'm on the right track.

5. Make a heartfelt commitment to seeing and feeling what's real. All of us want to feel comfortable, but striving for comfort can be a major trap. Some people are more committed to feeling good than they are to feeling what is real. Their real feelings start to emerge, and they drown them out with intellectual maneuvers or drugs or food.

People who try to feel good all the time often end up feeling bad most of the time. If you commit yourself to feeling what's real, you step out of this trap. Oddly enough, when you feel what's real, you end up feeling good most of the time.

I have a friend who tinkers with medicines and herbs constantly in an attempt to feel an elusive state of perfect well-being. It seems to me, though, that the more she tinkers the worse she feels. This is a predictable outcome, and not because of the medicines and herbs. It's because she focuses her attention on tiny downward fluctuations in the quality of her feeling of well-being. When this occurs, she takes some drops or a homeopathic pill to fix it. But there's a more fundamental law: what you put your attention on expands. The more sensitive she becomes to tinier fluctuations, the worse she will feel. She probably isn't actually in a worse state of health, but her inner feeling will tell her she is.

When I don't feel good, I look to the basics: Where am I out of integrity? What feelings am I denying, and what truths am I hiding? What needs to be loved in myself or others? It's important to use our state of well-being as a feedback system to tell us when we're drifting out of integrity. But it is equally important not to place demands on ourselves to feel comfortable all the time. There are plenty of times in life when feeling good in the long run requires that you sacrifice comfort in the short run. There are many things more important than feeling comfortable. I will list several, and you can add more from your own experience:

- Seeing and feeling what's real is more important than feeling comfortable. You may not feel good when you open that old closet and see the cobwebs and disarray. You may have a similar feeling of despair if you look at your life and find it a mess. However, to change ourselves we must first accept reality as it is. Then, by attending to reality in a loving and systematic way, we will eventually earn our good feelings, and they will be ours to keep.
- Keeping your agreements is more important than feeling comfortable. Many people do not keep their agreements because they want to get a little more sleep or finish dinner

or catch the crucial last few minutes of *Wheel of Fortune.* By trying to feel good at the expense of keeping agreements, they end up feeling bad.

- Telling the unarguable truth is more important than feeling comfortable. I have worked with thousands of people who delayed telling the truth about something because of a concern for "timing." In every case it turned out to be baloney. They were actually concerned with feeling bad when the other person got upset. They were trying to preserve comfort by not telling the truth.
- Working on your chosen life goals is more important than feeling comfortable. You won't feel good all the time while you are accomplishing your deathbed goals. Many of my goals cause me to stay up late, get up early, and get on airplanes to go places I wouldn't go otherwise. If I didn't do it I might get a little more sleep, but in the long run, the bad feelings of not moving toward my chosen goals would drag me down.

In contrast, the joy of moving toward my life goals is indescribable. As long as I stay centered and in touch with my friends and family, I find that I can work virtually tirelessly on my chosen projects. It doesn't matter whether it is an evening or a Sunday or a holiday. I don't really notice that I'm working because to me it is really not working at all. What would you call it when you're doing exactly what you want to do and having fun doing it? I'd call it play, and I would also call it the ultimate payoff for working on your self-esteem. I know at first hand what it feels like to feel bad about who I am, to not know what I want, and to spend all day working at a job I hate. Now for many years I have known the great joy of feeling at peace with myself, of being clear about my life path, and of moving in a centered way toward my goals. The deep and long-lasting feeling of well-being that all this work has produced has been well worth the occasional sacrifice of security and comfort.

In Summary

Discovering your true self opens a space in which you can feel harmony with yourself at the deepest level. When we're out of harmony with ourselves, genuine self-esteem is not possible. A car with a tiny misalignment in the front wheels can impart a frightful shimmy to all the riders. The joy of the journey is lost, and the possibility of getting to the goal is lessened. When we're in alignment—feeling and handling our fear, expressing the creativity that is within us, and in resonant harmony with our feelings—the journey becomes much smoother.

CHAPTER 7

How to Attract Lasting Love

In working with several thousand single and divorced people, Kathlyn and I have discovered that people often make three big inner shifts just before attracting a healthy new relationship into their lives. I too made similar shifts without being aware of them (at least consciously) just before I met Kathlyn. Once I made the shifts, it took only a month before she appeared in my life. In the years since we discovered the shifts, we've turned them into techniques, and we share these valuable secrets with thousands of people in our seminars. In this chapter I'll share them with you.

The techniques are simple but powerful. They work—if you do. From time to time you'll have to stop, think, fill in a blank, or do some other action step. My suggestion is, do it. Taking the action step will never require more than a matter of seconds, and

I can virtually guarantee that it will change your relationship destiny.

Those are strong words, but I've seen people turn their relationship destiny around so many times I have every confidence you can do it too. Speaking of strong words, you'll hear some from me in this chapter. I hope you'll permit me to speak to you straightforwardly, even bluntly at times. In order to attract genuine conscious love, we have to be extraordinarily gentle yet extraordinarily tough on ourselves. We have to love ourselves deeply and tenderly and yet at the same time be mercilessly demanding on ourselves in our commitment to a new kind of relationship. The stakes are high.

You may be one of those people who knows deep in your heart that you will never feel fulfilled until you have a conscious, loving relationship. I was, too, although it took me a long time to admit it. You may even have felt guilty for having that desire. For a long time I did, too. Desperately wanting a total and fulfilling love relationship was a guilty secret I carried buried inside myself for a long time. I'm glad I finally let myself want it, though, because it's not until we let ourselves consciously want something that we can consciously receive and enjoy it.

I congratulate you for keeping that desire alive. Until I was able to create the kind of relationship I have with Kathlyn, a little part of me was afraid that I was going to miss out on life's big prize. I'm glad I got the prize. It was worth the work and the wait.

The First Secret

There is one thing you absolutely must do if you want to attract genuine love into your life.

I had to do it. My wife had to do it.

The thousands of people I've helped create new love in their lives had to do it.

And you have to do it, too.

You need to make a *commitment* to attracting a new kind of relationship in your life. Nothing else but a soul-level commitment will do.

So let's not waste our time.

Do you want to attract a genuine, loving relationship into your life?

Are you ready and willing to make a full-scale commitment to something brand-new and completely satisfying?

If you do, if you really mean it, say Yes! out loud right now. (If you're in a public place you can whisper it!) But be sure to say it out loud. You've got to go public with a commitment for it to mean anything. If JFK hadn't gone public with a commitment to go to the moon, would we have gotten there? Maybe, but we'll never know. He had the courage to make a public commitment.

You've got to get your whole self into the commitment, because I've never seen anything succeed but total commitment.

You've got to want a new kind of relationship so deeply that you're willing to do whatever it takes to make it happen. If you're willing to make the commitment, you've done most of the work. The rest comes easy.

In a moment, I'm going to tell you specifically how to make the commitment to having a conscious relationship in your life.

First, though, you have to qualify.

You have to let yourself and the universe know that you are ready for a truly satisfying relationship.

You can qualify if you understand one key thing.

Listen carefully. Pay very close attention, because what I'm about to tell you will change every aspect of your life, starting with your relationships. It changed my life completely. I was never the same after I learned it. My whole life became radiant with new possibilities the moment I truly grasped it. I've watched the following awareness sink into thousands of people in audiences around the world, and the look on their faces let me know that their lives were changed forever.

Ready? Take a deep breath, and don't let it go until you've read the next sentence:

You are *already* getting what you're committed to getting.

Feel the truth of that statement, and let your breath go.

We *always* get what we're committed to getting.

If you're single and not liking it, you're *committed* to being single and not liking it. If you're divorced and afraid to get back into another relationship, you're *committed* to being divorced and afraid. Understand this point deep in your bones, and you finally understand how life works. *We're always getting what we're committed to getting!*

I'm not asking you to *like* this idea—I hated it when I first realized it and still don't like it sometimes now—but I do want you to acknowledge the truth of it. If you do, fill in the blank.

I, ____________________________, acknowledge that I always get what I'm committed to getting.

If you're like me (and practically every other human being on this planet), when you hear this piece of news every cell in your body starts screaming No! No! No!

We desperately want to believe that our intentions are one thing and what happens to us is another. When bad things happen to us repeatedly, we desperately want to believe it's not because we're *committed* to bad things happening to us. We close our eyes to the obvious truth, and then lo and behold, we keep the same patterns going.

But all the miserable losers I've ever met are committed to thinking that their intentions are different from what happens to them. In fact, that very way of thinking *makes* you a loser at the big game of life and love.

Don't get carried away with this idea and think that if you get one cold a year you're committed to getting colds. Colds happen—they're part of life on planet Earth—and if you get only one a year, good for you. But if you get sick a lot, you'd better start examining why you're committed to getting sick.

If you had one car wreck when you were a kid and have been a safe driver ever since, good for you. That means you're smart—you learn from your experience—and you don't need to worry about examining your commitment to having car accidents. But if you've had several accidents, if you keep getting dinged and fender bent, you'd better start examining your commitment to endangering yourself and others. I worked with a woman who'd had twenty-nine car accidents in her forty (dangerous) years on this planet. In one session she went from her loser thinking ("I guess it's just an unsafe world out there") to realizing that she was *committed* to endangering herself. Together we looked at where she might have picked up a commitment to having accidents, and she recited the usual childhood incidents of not being wanted and loved. But the past is never the point. I've never seen anyone change their lives by talking about the past, and if you talk about it longer than ten minutes you're wasting major time.

Talking about the past only helps if you turn on a dime and make a brand-new commitment. She turned her life around by making a forward flip into a new commitment. I invited her to say: "I acknowledge that I'm presently committed to endangering myself and others, and I now consciously commit to producing safety everywhere I go."

We worked on that commitment until she felt it deep in her bones. When she walked out of that session she was a different person, and in thirteen years she has never had another car wreck. All this remarkable turnaround came from the split second when she chose to acknowledge her commitment to endangering herself and others and chose to make a new commitment that was stronger.

If you smoked cigarettes for a while then quit because it was making you sick, good for you. You caught on quick. But if you're still smoking (or drinking or stuffing yourself with dead foods that make you fat, nervous, or tired), you better examine your commitment to killing yourself.

I had to do it, and you do, too. I can say that because I'm a former fat smoker (300 pounds, two packs of Marlboros a day) who endured four years of a horrible first marriage before I caught on.

Now I weigh what I ought to weigh for my height (6'1", 180 pounds), I haven't had a smoke in almost thirty years, and I've created and maintained a glorious conscious relationship for two decades. From that, I can reasonably conclude that I'm committed to having health and love in my life.

Why is this point so important? It's because you need the energy from this awareness to fuel your commitment to a new kind of relationship. The moment you understand that you're committed to things being the way they are now, you unleash a powerful force that will give a rocket ride to your new commitment.

If you're single, fill in the following sentence:

Right now I, ______________________________, am committed to being single.

How do we know you're committed to being single? Because you're single, that's why. You always get what you're committed to getting.

If you're divorced, fill in the following sentence:

Right now I, ______________________________, am committed to being divorced.

How do we know you're committed to being divorced? Because you're divorced.

If you're in an unhappy relationship right now, fill in the blank:

Right now I, ______________________________, am committed to being in an unhappy relationship.

You keep your life exquisitely simple by realizing you get whatever you're committed to getting. You make your life miserable and complicated by proclaiming that you're not getting what you're committed to getting. If you whine, "I'm single but I'm really committed to being married," you waste your precious energy.

The moment you realize that the way it is right now is the way you want it (usually on some unconscious level), you unleash a powerful force, the same power that will carry you to a new positive commitment that has nothing—repeat, nothing!—to do with your past.

If you're single or divorced or in an unhappy relationship right now, and if you want to be in a new conscious relationship, repeat after me: "I'm committed to things being the way they are right now, and I make a new, conscious commitment to creating a new, conscious relationship."

Standing where you are, do an imaginary soul flip into a new commitment, and fill in the blank:

I, ______________________________, make a conscious new commitment to enjoying a conscious, loving relationship with a conscious, loving __________ (man or woman).

Flash back to 1979, where I am sitting, stunned and speechless, on the floor of my apartment. I have just had the most painful and illuminating conversation of my entire life.

During an argument with my lover of five years, I suddenly realize that it's not our several hundredth argument. It's our several hundredth run-through of the *same* argument. A lightbulb comes on, a beam of awareness shines down on me, and I see clearly that our arguments always follow the same pattern of misery-producing moves.

The First Move: One of us doesn't tell the truth about something. Usually it's something trivial we hide, like "I was angry when you came home late." Sometimes it's something more substantial, like the time she didn't tell me she'd started using drugs again after promising me she'd never do it again. Or the time I neglected to tell her about a one-night sexual encounter I'd had.

The Second Move: One of us makes a confrontation, such as, "You're acting sort of strange. Is there anything you haven't told me?"

The Third Move: One of us stonewalls: "Nope, everything's fine."

The Fourth Move: Somebody escalates by blaming, claiming victim status, or sputtering with righteous indignation: "You always say that! Can't you once just tell the truth? I don't know why I put up with this kind of . . ."

It whips up into a furious crescendo and eventually dies down, three days later. For some strange reason it usually takes three days to wind down.

But on this magic occasion, I caught it before it went into spin cycle.

I stepped back from the process and saw the pattern for the first time. I shifted into an altered state of consciousness, as if I were watching both of us from a distance. The lucid part of me wondered, why would I engage in a pattern like this? Given all the experiences I could be having as a human being, why did I keep repeating the pattern of lying and being lied to, being criticized and criticizing, blaming and being blamed, thinking of myself as a victim?

Then, in a rush of ecstatic realization, I got the answer. These things kept happening because I was *committed* to being criticized, *committed* to being betrayed, *committed* to arguing and lying. I was more committed to them than I was to being close.

The moment I realized what my commitment was, I felt a shift. Another part of me wondered, why would you be committed to this kind of pain?

Immediately the answer came through, from some wise part of me: because I was engaged in this drama from the moment of my conception! The drama of my conception involved my father's betrayal of my mother, her shame and fury and hatred of being pregnant. In a sense, my existence ruined my mother's life, and I don't think she ever forgave herself, my father, and, by extension, me for getting her into the mess. All the elements of the drama were there when I walked into the party. By the time I could think for myself (or even walk by myself), I had already been pickled in this drama for years.

Now for some bad news: so were you.

Now for the good news: there's an easy way out.

I imagine you've figured out why I'm telling you all this. It's because I want to save you a lot of trouble. I want you to acknowledge that whatever painful drama of relationship you live in is one you've been committed to body and soul, but *not because you ever made a conscious commitment to it.* Your relationship drama, like mine, was an unconscious commitment you and I made because it came with something you desperately wanted: a ticket to the food supply. It was part of the air you breathed.

None of us has the slightest chance of a healthy relationship until we make a *conscious* commitment to it. Now for the truly good news. Making a commitment—a genuine, heartfelt, soul-shifting commitment—takes no effort whatsoever. Once you do it, there are some things you'll need to learn and some moves you'll have to make under pressure, but the actual making of the commitment is something you do inside yourself, with no effort whatsoever.

So, how about it? Do you commit, body and soul, to living your life-expanding waves of consciousness and love? Or, by default, do you commit to perpetuating whatever drama you've been engaged in for the last umpteen years since you first sucked air?

It's that simple.

Right now, commit to one or the other.

Fill in the blank:

I, ____________________________, commit to living my life in expanding waves of love and consciousness.

or

I, ____________________________, commit to perpetuating the painful drama I've been engaged in for much of my life.

If you have made the first commitment, you're ready to move—fast. If you made the second, come back and try again later.

The Second Secret

We live in a three-dimensional world, and there are probably lots more dimensions we haven't mapped out yet. We know for sure that we live in at least three dimensions.

You know that you are high, wide, and deep. You might be five feet tall and two feet wide, or you might be six feet tall and sixteen inches wide. For the purposes of creating a conscious relationship, it doesn't matter how high you are or how wide you are, but it matters a lot how deep you are. If you have depth (or presence or spirit or whatever you want to call it), you can lead a magnificent life. If you don't have depth, you can be the perfect height and width and still be miserable.

When you embark on creating a conscious, loving relationship, you need to consider depth—your own depth and the depth of the person you want to spend your life with.

For me, deeper is better. I love depth, in myself and in the people I hang around with. My wife has incredible depths to her. Because of this, each year she becomes more beautiful to be with and more treasured by me and her friends. She feels deeply, she sees deeply into people, she touches a piece of lettuce with the same depth with which she writes a poem. I'm inspired by the depth of her, and I strive to live and love from so deep a place in myself.

So, deep—really deep—works for me. However, the depth you want to live at is completely up to you. All I'm asking is that when you create a conscious, loving relationship, you put some consideration into depth.

Height and width are important, too. Unless you're superhuman, you have some preferences about height and weight and width. For example, I prefer women more toward the zaftig end of the spectrum. My wife could get a job as a belly dancer but wouldn't get a nod as a runway model. And that's fine with me. Before I met Kathlyn, I enjoyed relationships—even passionate ones—with women who looked like fashion models, but it's always been because of the depths, not because of the height or width. When I finally met my soul mate—with her incredible heart and spirit wrapped in a richly contoured body—I felt I'd died and gone to heaven. Two decades later I still feel that way. I can't believe my good fortune, and all she has to do to turn me on, body and soul, is walk into the room.

But all considerations of height and weight are individual to you. If you want a poster child for anorexia, good for you. If you want pumped pecs in a Speedo suit, fine with me. If you want a skinny Calvin clone with a sullen pout and a tattooed tush, blessings on you. All I ask is that you give some consideration to depth.

So, when you form your picture of the person you'd like to be with, spend a few moments considering that character, according to Dwight Moody, is what we are in the dark. When the lights are off, when the belly dancer and the anorexic and the pumped pecs are hidden from view, you and the person next to you are simply depth. There, in the silence, when the room lights are off, how much inner light is still on?

That's a very important question, because some day the pecs will deflate, the tattoo will fade, and the belly dancer contours will lose their definition. Then depth becomes incredibly important. The most miserable people I've met are those who do not have a rich inner life and a flowing sense of connection with others to sustain them as they age.

Okay, you see where I'm coming from.

Now to the specifics:

What are your Absolute Yeses and your Absolute Nos?

What are three things you absolutely must have in a mate? What are three things that you want to celebrate every moment of every day? Your Absolute Yeses are not just things you want, they are also things you cherish and wish to celebrate. Imagine waking up in the morning and celebrating with a resounding cheer of "Yes!" What would the "Yes!" be celebrating? For me, when I wake up in the morning and realize I get to live another day in a relationship of authenticity, integrity, and creativity, that's worth celebrating!

I want you to find out what would be so great that you would wake up celebrating it every day.

Now for your Nos. What are three things you absolutely will not put up with? What are three things you will wake up celebrating that you successfully eliminated from your relationship life? For me, it's worth celebrating every day that I eliminated my need to save addicts from their fate. It never worked anyway. They never said, "Thanks to you, I have decided to eliminate alcohol and drugs from my life." In fact, they usually ripped off my time and energy (and occasionally other stuff), wrecked my cars, broke promises, and conspired with me to turn my life into a never-ending melodrama on my own private twenty-four-hour-a-day soap opera, *As the Stomach Turns.*

Now I can wake up every day celebrating that I have successfully switched that channel off and kept it off for twenty years. Yes!

I want to know what you so much don't want in your life that you will wake up celebrating that you successfully eliminated it.

While you're thinking, let me share my own absolutes.

Flash back to that fateful moment in 1979. I realized that the absolute most important thing to me was honesty. I didn't want to spend another minute of my life concealing things from myself or anybody else.

I didn't want to spend another minute being with someone who was concealing something from me. I wanted to make sure I never had another conversation that went:

ME: What's going on? You look upset.

OTHER PERSON: No, I'm just fine. (Then, three hours later the truth comes out about what the person was upset about all along.)

This was a conversation that went on with various members of my original family on many hundreds of occasions. I must have internalized the need for it so thoroughly that I simply transferred it over to women in my adult life.

I realized I needed to make such a strong commitment to honesty that it formed a field around me that repelled dishonest people and invited only honest ones in.

So I did. I said to the universe, "I commit to a relationship with a woman who's totally honest. I commit myself to unflinching honesty with myself and others, and I commit to inviting only honest people into my life."

That was my first Absolute Yes.

Your first Absolute Yes should be the most important thing you require in a relationship. And that begins with your relationship with yourself. I figured that if I were completely honest with myself, it would give strength and validity to my request for an honest relationship.

It's important that your Absolute Yes be something that you want for yourself as well as from others. If your Absolute Yes is for beauty, for example, you need to be sure you are in touch with the beauty in yourself. You can't demand something of another person that you haven't given yourself.

My second Absolute Yes was: "I commit to a relationship with a woman who takes total responsibility for her life, her feelings, and what happens to her. I commit to taking total responsibility for my own life, my feelings, and what happens to me."

My third Absolute Yes: "I commit to a relationship with a woman who has her own creative path and one that's harmonious with mine."

This commitment was important to me because I had struggled in past relationships with partners who were envious of my commitment to my creative path. My first wife was not a reader, for example, and often criticized me for spending time reading. In my life, though, sitting around reading is not a luxury, it's an absolute fundamental requirement for my well-being. Another lover was jealous of the success of my first book. After feeling victimized by this, I finally woke up and took responsibility for creating this reaction: I realized that if I were thoroughly committed to my own creativity, I wouldn't create resistance to it. Resistance was simply evidence of my internal resistance to embracing my creativity fully.

Now for my Absolute Nos.

I said no to ever again being in relationship with someone with an active addiction. If the person used any tobacco, alcohol, or other drugs on a regular basis, I didn't want to have a close relationship with that person. My mother had died from her drug addiction, and her practice of it had made my childhood chaotic. Based on this programming, in my early twenties I had gone out and married an alcoholic. Then, after going through great pains to divorce her four years later, I took up with a woman who was addicted to tobacco, alcohol, and Valium. Call me a slow learner.

My second Absolute No was to vow never again to enter a relationship with a Blamer. Based on her experiences with thousands of families, the gifted therapist Virginia Satir divided people into five groups: Levelers, Blamers, Placaters, Super-Reasonables, and Distracters.

Levelers will tell you what's going on with them in a straightforward way, and they will listen to you compassionately if you level with them. They're easy to be around, because they know that when people level with each other their natural love and goodness will come forth. They know that having a good time and helping others have a good time is what life's all about. Every moment they get the same choice everybody else does—the choice between loving and creating melodramas based on fear—and they choose love.

Blamers think you're responsible for their pain, and they won't take any responsibility for the pain they create. They believe that the one who finds the most fault wins. You can't win with a Blamer, and as a result they're a pain to be around.

Placaters are always looking to please, but it's a desire to please that's based on fear. They're afraid of disapproval, so they do whatever they can to avoid it. Usually they sacrifice their relationship with themselves in the service of pleasing others, then they feel a deep resentment about the sacrifice. They are the chameleons of the relationship world; you never know quite what their true color is, and neither do they.

Super-Reasonables are cut off from their feelings, believing that cool logic is the only way to operate. They pooh-pooh emotions, they're convinced they're right about all things, and they spend a lot of their time trying to convince you of it. They believe that the one who dies with the tightest ass wins. They're a pain to be around.

Distracters are always changing the subject and creating uproars. If they can't win, they like to mess up the game so nobody else can. They believe the person who creates the biggest drama wins, regardless of who loses in the process. They're a pain to be around.

Some people are combinations of two or more of the above.

As I sat there on my floor in 1979, age thirty-four, counting up the romantic relationships of my adult life, my scorecard looked like this:

3 Blamers
1 Super-Reasonable
1 Distracter
2 Combo Platters
1 Leveler

Unfortunately for me (but to her great credit), my one Leveler had spent a frustrating couple of years with me, then dropped me like a hot spud.

My scorecard revealed that I had a bad habit of attracting Blamers. I decided to say no to that pattern. I committed to being unwaveringly vigilant for any Blamers who strayed into my path.

My third Absolute No was to vow never again to form a relationship with a Shirker. Shirkers are people who don't like to do their share of the work, whatever it is. I had learned the hard way that everybody fundamentally wears one of two T-shirts. One T-shirt has "What Can I Get?" written on the front, the other has "What Can I Do to Help?" Earlier in my life, I attracted people who wore a Get-Shirt, then I wasted my energy complaining about having to do all the work. But who was the sucker that kept inviting them into his life in the first place? That would, er, uh, be me.

After you form your Absolute Yeses and Absolute Nos, you get to express your preferences. That's where you get to place your order for a belly dancer rather than a waif. First, though, you need to be clear about your absolutes.

So do that right now. It should take you no longer than ten minutes. If you take longer than ten minutes, you're likely to be kidding yourself or avoiding thinking about it.

Take a deep breath, and muster the courage to ask yourself: What is my first Absolute Yes? What is the absolute most important thing I require in a relationship? What do I want to celebrate every moment of every day?

Write it down.

The most important thing I require and want to celebrate in a relationship is ____

____.

What is your second Absolute Yes?

The second most important thing I require and want to celebrate in a relationship is ____

____.

The third most important thing I require and want to celebrate in a relationship is ____

____.

Now let's work on your Absolute Nos.

The most important thing I vow never to invite into my life again is ______

____.

The second most important thing I vow never to invite into my life is ___

____.

The third most important thing I vow never to invite into my life is ______

____.

Now let's float some preferences out into the ether. What turns you on? If you had your proverbial druthers, what would you prefer?

Think of the universe as a big, smiling cosmic waitress or waiter, just waiting to take your order. Go ahead, place it.

Tell the universe exactly what you'd like.

In a Manhattan restaurant awhile back, the waiter asked me what I'd like for breakfast. Blueberry pancakes, I said, and can you please ask the chef to make them with love?

For a split second a look of utter astonishment crossed his face, then he burst out laughing.

"I think we can do that," he said.

When my pancakes came, they were signed by the chef, in blueberry syrup, "With love, Andre."

Unless we ask for what we want, the universe doesn't have a chance to give it to us. In return for this great gift of life, don't we owe the universe the gift of letting it know how it can please us?

It's okay to be pleased. It's glorious to please.

Sit back for a moment and let's wonder together: what's your pleasure?

The Third Secret

I'll give you the punch line up front. The thing that keeps people from forming and keeping great relationships is an unloved part of themselves. We don't love some part of ourselves, and in desperation we run around trying to get someone else to love us in hopes that if they give us enough love our unlovable part will go away. It never does. Only a moment of loving ourselves unconditionally will do it.

Although most of us have spent a lifetime running from that unlovable part of us, when we finally confront it we discover it's a fear, and any fear is simply a pulsating quiver of racy queasy sensations in your stomach area. As we saw in chapter 6, fear is merely excitement without the breath. Breathe into the fear, and the butterflies will flutter out of hiding and fly away.

When we love that fear directly—a split second of love is all it needs—the fear disappears and we open a vast space into which the great relationships of our lives can enter.

Until we give that scary place in ourselves a split second of love, it's impossible to enjoy good relationships. The reason: the fear causes us to push away the very aspects of ourselves that most need love. Then we try to make up for that lack by getting other people to love us. Trying to get other people to love us—when we don't think ourselves lovable—is like a dog chasing its own tail. The more they love us, the faster we run from it.

Pause right now, and love the place in yourself that's hardest to love.

Maybe it's your fear of being alone.

Or maybe it's your fear that nobody will love you because your face is ugly.

Perhaps it's something you did in the past that's hardest for you to love.

There's always something we haven't loved, and the most beautiful of the "beautiful people" I've worked with have more unlovable places in themselves than the average person on the street. You're not alone.

For me, the hardest place inside to love was a deep fear that was accompanied by anger and grief. After some unflinching self-inquiry, I discovered that fear of abandonment ran every destructive program I operated, from binge eating to pushing away people who were trying to love me. Based on events in my first year of life, I felt afraid of being left to die, and this fear gave rise to a host of other problems.

The two most troublesome ones were my eating disorder and my habit of pushing away love. I ate to quell my fear, and this habit made me a three hundred pounder by the time I was in my twenties. I also rejected people who were trying to help me; later I discovered that I pushed them away so they wouldn't leave me. If I pushed them away, my crazy mind figured, I would be in control of the leaving.

A fat person who pushed away love! Not exactly the kind of slogan I wanted chiseled on my tombstone! So I radically rewrote my life script. I went on a diet of mainly fruits and vegetables, lost a hundred pounds, and felt fabulous. The other diet I put myself on was much harder to maintain: I quit pushing away love. I accepted help. I told people my feelings. I quit pretending I knew everything. As if by magic, a world of love opened up before me. Soon I was surrounded by love, completely encircled by it. It had been there all the time, waiting for me to change my mind and let it in.

That's what I want you to do right now.

Take a deep breath, and imagine filling yourself with love. Love yourself deeply for all the things you find unlovable about yourself.

Don't think about it—it's unthinkable.

Just love. In fact, the thinking part of your mind doesn't want you to do what I'm inviting you to do. If you don't love yourself, your ego can stay in control one more day. Your ego eats the unloved parts of you for breakfast every day and stays pumped up with glee by every self-critical thought you crank through your mind.

So don't think about it. Jump out into the freedom of the unknown, and love yourself deeply. Love yourself for not knowing exactly how to love yourself.

And keep returning to love. It's the big safety net of the universe.

Action

Do a quick-change act right this minute. Slip out of your ego—it never really fit you, anyway—and stand up straight in your rebirthday suit. Rebirth yourself right now by writing down as many things as you can think of that are hard for you to love about yourself.

____

____

____

____

____

____

____

____

____

When you've got your list, go through and love each of those things in yourself. Be with each of them for a few seconds in a spirit of loving acceptance. Love them deeply in yourself so you will not require anyone to love them for you.

Remember the punch line I gave you earlier? Let me say it again a slightly different way. If you don't love yourself, you'll always be looking for someone to do it for you. And you won't ever find it, because people who don't love themselves attract people who don't love themselves.

When you love yourself, deeply and unconditionally and for everything you are and aren't, you attract people who love themselves. Then your relationships become partnerships on the path of love, a real playground of limitless possibility.

I like thinking of life and love as a vast playground. For me, life is best when it's done in a spirit of play. I'm sure that many would disagree, but I feel fine about that because I'm also sure I'm having a better time than they are! Diane Ackerman, in a beautiful book called *Deep Play,* points out that the whole human saga evolved through play. Ideas reverberate playfully in the mind; I toss and turn these words playfully until I get them the way I want them. I glance up from the words and watch two squirrels madly chasing each other around my lawn, bent on some demented game with its own rules. Up and down the scale, play defines us. So let's think of the great game of creating conscious love as the best play we can imagine on the best playground of all.

On the playground of conscious relationships, everybody gets to play, everybody gets to win, everybody gets to go home with the prize. All you have to do is follow the playground rules, and the good stuff naturally happens. The rules are simple and based on how the universe works. We didn't make them up, we inherited them. Maybe nobody told you what they were when you were a kid. Don't worry, they didn't tell me, either.

Here they are.

Rule One: Be Real

If you are completely authentic with yourself, you'll stay in a naturally good mood as you walk around in the world. If you tell the authentic truth to other people, you'll have clear relationships with them. If you don't, things will get seriously out of control very quickly. To get back in the flow of harmony, all you have to do is look and see where you stopped telling the truth to yourself or someone else. Return to where the blip occurred, and fix it by telling the truth.

In other words, if your car starts shimmying on the highway, look for the wheel that's out of alignment and true it up. It doesn't take much of a misalignment to get one whale of a shimmy, especially if you're whizzing along at a rapid clip.

If your life stops working, look for a simple truth you "forgot" to tell.

If you look underneath any major mess anyone's created in his or her life, you will usually find a truth that didn't get told, a truth that usually would take less than ten seconds to tell.

Pop Quiz: What is a simple truth that would have restored integrity to O. J. Simpson's life?

Hint: It would take less than ten seconds to speak it.

Pop Quiz: Remember Richard Nixon? He denied any knowledge of Watergate and ended up getting run out of office. I'll bet if he'd told the ten-second truth—"Yep, I knew about that, and I feel colossally stupid for being part of it"—he would have been beat up for a little while, then forgiven. But he stonewalled, got caught, and ended up having to sneak out like a weasel.

Then there was George Bush, who said "Read my lips—no new taxes." Then he went ahead and raised taxes. Good-bye, George. Then along comes Bill. That would be Bill "I never had sex with that woman" Clinton. He not only told a colossal lie, he got coached by his Hollywood friends on how to clench his jaw and shake his finger while he was lying so he could sell it better. So much for getting coached by professional liars.

You get the point.

Now let's get down to the nitty-gritty:

What is one thing you have difficulty speaking about authentically with others? ______________________________

____

What's another? ____

____

What's something that you haven't told the truth about in your life? Something that would restore integrity to your life if you came clean about it? ____

____

On the big playground of conscious relationship, absolute authenticity is required. If you do not tell the truth, you forfeit your right to romance. Get as comfortable telling the truth as you are with walking in the sunshine on the beach on a beautiful day. Your whole life becomes a walk on the beach on a beautiful day when you become impeccable about telling the truth.

Rule Two: Be Appreciative

A grateful heart is a glorious thing to carry around inside you. Gratitude feels absolutely wonderful. However, other people don't get to enjoy it unless you speak your gratitude out loud. If you lead with appreciation—actually start conversations off with appreciations throughout the day—you'll create a field of positive energy around you wherever you go.

As you're walking down the street with a friend, you may notice the sunlight glinting on the fresh dew (as I did this morning). Open your mouth and say, "Right now I'm appreciating how the sunlight looks glinting on the dew." That's all it takes to put you in the flow of appreciation.

At first people may think you're a little odd, but that's simply because they aren't used to living in a world in which people take the time to appreciate things. We've got to create that sort of world. Otherwise, people will just keep on walking around with their shoulders tight, wincing from the last blast of negative energy and cringing in anticipation of the next one. Let's create a new world in which people look for what's right as well as what's wrong, a world in which we speak the simple truths about what we appreciate about ourselves, our companions, our world.

Right now, look around you and let your eyes rest on something you can appreciate.

Then, fill in the blank with your appreciation:

I appreciate____
____.

Keep the flow going with some even deeper appreciations:

One of the biggest appreciations I have about life on earth is __________
____.

I deeply appreciate myself for the way I ___________________________
____.

(Thinking of someone you're intimate with) I deeply appreciate ______________ for the way he/she ___________________________.

Rule Three: Listen Without Interrupting People

Breathe while you're listening to people. Give breathing space to their speaking. Pause briefly after they finish speaking *before* you rush in with your point of view. People especially like it when you give them an informal summary of what they've said. A friend of mine went to a party where he knew no one. He decided that, rather than trying to impress any of these new people, he would spend the evening simply listening to them and summarizing what they said. He went through several hours saying things like "If I understand what you're saying, you . . ." and "Let me see if I've got what you mean . . ." At the end of the party several people mentioned to his wife about what a remarkable person he was. The word *charismatic* was used by one person to describe him, while another called him one of the most articulate people she'd ever met. Could it be that charisma and brilliance have as much to do with how we listen as what we say?

Imagine a world in which people actually listened to one another rather than just waiting for other people to stop talking so they could give their opinion.

Let's make it happen. After all, who owns the playground?

Close your eyes, take a few breaths, and give a simple summary of what you've just learned in the past minute.

Rule Four: Practice Impeccable Agreements

Here's how to keep your life simple and flowing with miracles: do what you say you're going to do. Don't do what you say you're not going to do.

If you find you can't deliver on a promise or keep an agreement, have a conscious conversation with the person and change the agreement. Make amends for the broken promise. Nobody's perfect. Let's all get busy creating a world in which we strive for impeccability, make amends when we fall short, and get back up and go again.

Think back over the last couple of days:

One example of my impeccability—doing what I said I was going to do—is ____.

One example of less than impeccability—not doing what I said I was going to do, or doing something I said I wouldn't do—is ______________________
____.

One person I need to make amends with is ______________________
____.

Those are the rules. From thirty years of working with people, and from twenty years of living and loving in a conscious relationship with Kathlyn, I can tell you from painful experience that you will blow any chances of a conscious relationship by breaking them. Because the rules of conscious relationship are the same rules that run the universe itself, you'll get busted even if you're not in a close relationship. Tough talk, perhaps, but I'd sure want any friend of mine to know it.

If you follow the rules, though, you get to have the best time that's available on our fine planet. You get to live with a flow of well-being coursing through your body, a feeling of connection with loving people around you, and a direct pipeline to the creative juices of the universe.

What a deal!

Now, for some nitty-gritty details of how to go about creating a conscious relationship on a daily basis.

Making It Happen *Now!*

Quick, make a decision: Do you want to create a conscious relationship now? Or do you want to wait until later? Either one is fine with me; I put it off for thirty-four years before I decided to do it.

Pick one.

If you picked *Now!* keep reading.

If you decided to wait until later, you can wait to do this lesson until you're ready for Now!

Okay, if you're still reading, I'm going to assume you picked Now! From here on out I'm going to call you a Now! Person.

From here on I want you to play full-out.

Awhile back I walked past a basketball court and saw a bunch of folks in wheelchairs careening around the court, playing a full-out game of basketball. They were sweating, hollering, cheering, and having a heck of a time. Nearby, stretched out on the grass, sat some teenagers, puffing on cigarettes, guzzling pop, and making smart-ass put-downs of the basketball players.

I paused to take note. Here, I thought, I'm seeing the very essence of what I love most and love least about human beings, myself included.

I love seeing a bunch of people in wheelchairs whipping around a basketball court, using all the resources they've been given, and taking it out to the edge. I think it sucks when I see people with good legs sitting on their asses, people with the gift of human speech wasting that gift on sarcastic commentary.

Now! People take whatever they're given and create a thrilling, magnificent life by virtue of their commitment.

Now! People play full-out.

Now! People have goals, and I want you to play full-out in the direction of your chosen goals. Everybody else has goals, too. If our goals are simply to suck air through our nose or push food in the top end of our tube and squeeze it out the bottom later, those are still goals.

Now! People have goals they've carefully chosen.

People with conscious goals are sexier. Couples with conscious goals are happier. It's okay to have financial goals, spiritual goals, whatever kind of goals you want. It's okay even to have a goal of not having goals all the time. Sometimes I like to space out, lie about, goof off, and not have any goals for a while. You might say I place a high value on not producing any value from time to time.

You've chosen to be a Now! Person, and you've chosen the goal of creating a conscious relationship. Here's what I want you to do every day for a week to show you mean it.

Every hour you're awake, I want you to do three things, none of which takes longer than ten seconds. Post a reminder to yourself to do them. Do them for a week, and you will create such remarkable magic around you that I predict you'll have a hard time believing your own power.

Each of these three ten-second moves is so simple that later you'll look back on them and wonder, "How could something that simple change my relationship destiny so quickly?"

It's because each one of them, though simple, is utterly outrageous. You'll see.

The First Ten-Second Move

The first thing I want you to do is float a positive thought through your mind every hour. Once each hour think, "I enjoy conscious, loving relationships everywhere I go."

Notice that the thought is in the present tense. You're a Now! Person, so you're saying you enjoy this kind of relationship Now!

Say it a few times in your mind right now. Get the feeling of it. Get so you enjoy the feeling of it.

Whether or not you feel like it, simply circulate the thought through your mind every hour.

Post reminders in key locations, such as your dashboard, your mirrors, your computer.

The Second Ten-Second Move

Say something authentic every hour. Once an hour, speak one authentic sentence. Of course, I hope you'll speak hundreds, but start with one an hour.

Here are a few from my last couple of hours.

To my wife, across the room: "I'm happy." I had just felt a delicious blissful feeling tickling around in my stomach. She looked up at me, smiled, and went back to reading her book.

To the clerk at the deli counter: "I like the way all these are laid out. I feel hungry just looking at them." I had just noticed how all the pastries and muffins were arranged, obviously with care and attention to aesthetics. She registered surprise, then smiled broadly. "Thanks," she said, "I did that myself."

"Still sore, but better today than yesterday." My wife had just asked me how my mouth felt. I recently had some dental work, from which the inside of my mouth is healing.

None of these things is particularly profound, and that's just fine. We're not looking for profound, just simple and frequent. Profound may happen from time to time, but first we have to retrain ourselves to be reliably real.

Start with one an hour, and work toward that 100 percent mark. Just as I'm doing.

The Third Ten-Second Move

Speak an appreciation once an hour. Each hour, open your heart and your mouth at the same time.

Here are some things you can start with:

Appreciate your family and friends. "John, I appreciate how I can count on you to do what you say you're going to do."

"Sally, I appreciate the attention you give the new kitten."

"Sandy, I appreciate how your voice sounds."

Keep your appreciations simple. Again, we're not going for profound here, just frequent and real.

We're training ourselves to look for what's right, what's good, what's working. We're training ourselves to look for what we're grateful for and to speak our gratitude to others.

In a lecture awhile back I was talking about giving one appreciation an hour, and a tight, hostile-looking person took the mike and asked sarcastically, "So we're supposed to go around gushing all over the furniture all the time?"

I had to laugh, as did most of the audience. You've got a problem with your nozzle if you think that one ten-second appreciation per hour qualifies as gushing. There are 360 ten-second chunks of time in every hour. All I want you to do, at first, is to take one of the 360 chunks and speak an appreciation in it. Soon, perhaps, we'll be wanting to speak appreciations in ten or twenty of those ten-second blocks, but let's start with one. I've never seen that harm the furniture in any way.

CHAPTER 8

How to Create Thriving Relationships and Conscious Sex

Relationships are difficult for all of us some of the time and for some of us all the time. The relationship journey is even more perilous because most of us don't get any useful education on the subject. I was schooled in a time when there was not a single hour during the twelve years of primary and secondary education devoted to any of the skills of close relationship. Such skills as listening, problem solving, commitment, and communication were left entirely to chance. The most significant aspect of our lives is left to default, when the barest attention to design would yield enormous benefits in happiness and well-being.

The power of relationship is caused by something simple but profound. When you reach out to touch another person, you are touching the whole universe. You are the universe touching itself. The universe is a whole, and it also has individual parts. Although we may think of ourselves as individual parts, we are always in relationship to the wholeness of ourselves, others, and the world around us. In relationships with other people, we must embrace the wholeness not only of them but of ourselves. This is indeed a challenge, one we are dealing with before we know it.

From conception onward, our lives are about relationship. Relationship is who we are and what we do. The whole universe is actually the sum total of our relationships with one another. What we think of as "the world" is really our relationships. It's all we know. They tell us the universe began with a big bang—for sure, our own personal universe begins with a miniature replay of this explosive moment.

Following the union of sperm and egg, the process of individuation begins immediately and continues throughout life. We become our individual selves within the context of relationship. If we become conscious of who we are and what we do in relationship, we have a chance to be happy and to contribute to others' happiness. If not—if we take the default alternative of unconscious relationship—there is little chance that we can create happiness. There is, in fact, a high likelihood that we will create and perpetuate misery for ourselves and others around us. That is why conscious relationship is a required course of life. We are already enrolled; our only choice is whether to stay awake and learn.

The process of union and individuation continues during our development. You and I were in union with our mothers while we were inside them, but we were also individuating with blinding speed. Then later, although we were in union with the breast or in someone's arms with a bottle, we were also becoming separate and autonomous while at the same time being nurtured in unity. From the very beginning the two driving pulsations of our lives are union and individuation. And this pulsation continues throughout our lives. Life is not a success for us unless we can resonate in union with others and with ourselves in full autonomy.

My Relationship Journey

I don't remember having a single thought about creating a conscious relationship until I was thirty-four years old. Up until one turning point in 1979, I simply sailed through relationships at whim, propelled by the shifting winds of chance and my unconscious programming. Sometimes I feel embarrassed that it took this long; at other times I feel grateful it happened at all. Once I figured out what I wanted and made a commitment to it, it took me only a month to manifest a relationship of incredible joy and wonder. Of course, once Kathlyn came into my life we both needed to dedicate ourselves to making it work on a daily basis. But I now know from personal experience that it is possible to do two things: to create a relationship by design instead of default, and to learn the powerfully simple skills necessary to maintain its creative potential over the long term.

My first insight into the difficulties of relationship came when I was ten. I was riding in the backseat of my grandparents' '37 Chevrolet, the kind with running boards and the headlights perched on top of the fenders. The car was about twenty years old when the incident I'm about to describe occurred.

My grandmother was driving my grandfather home from work. In the early days of the automobile, my grandfather had taken a position that cars were a passing fad and a dangerous one at that. He did not want to waste his precious time learning about them. He had stolen a mule to run away from home in 1890 when he was a teen, and he had driven a buggy to Florida in 1902 with my grandmother riding shotgun.

The invention of the automobile signaled a speeding up of life that he much disapproved of, and although he lived to see the first moon walk, he was a reluctant participant in the mechanical era. His antidriving stance forced my grandmother to drive him everywhere, a job she performed with sullen reluctance. As a driver, she had her own eccentricities. The main one continues to be unique in my experience: she refused to drive in reverse. No one knows how she came to this odd prejudice, but I can remember occasions after I got my driver's license when I had to bail her out of parking jams where only the reverse gear could be used. I'm not making this up.

Back to the moment when I was ten. On this day I asked about something I'd noticed dozens of times, a streak that ran down the passenger-side window. "What is that big brown streak running down the window? How come it doesn't come off when we wash it?"

The backs of my grandparents' necks stiffened at this question. The car chugged along for a couple of blocks, my grandparents locked in tight-jawed silence. Seeing that I had trod on dangerous ground, I quickly changed the subject. Later I got the story from each side.

They had been out for a spin in the car the week it was new, long before I was born. Bear with me for a moment as I tell you a disgusting but key detail: my grandfather chewed tobacco, a habit that my grandmother absolutely loathed. This habit required him to make a sound like "Patooey" every minute or so, as a stream of brown tobacco juice arched out of his mouth. Usually, he was uncannily accurate with this projectile; I can still hear the "ping" of it hitting the can he used as a spittoon.

He worked his cud of tobacco as the new car spun along on its inaugural ride. The window on his side was new and pristine, and he mistakenly thought it was rolled down. He turned his head, went "Patooey," and let fly. Unfortunately, the window was up, and the tobacco juice hit the window with a massive "splat." A huge uproar ensued about who was going to clean it off. My grandmother's position was that he should be the one to clean it off. After all, he spat it there. My grandfather's position was, he didn't do windows! That was women's work. Besides, he hadn't really wanted to go along with this car business in the first place, anyhow.

They entrenched themselves in their respective positions, and eighteen years later the streak was still there. You can see from this incident why the subject of creating conscious relationships is sacred to me.

At this writing, Kathlyn and I have been together about twenty years. I was born in 1945, so we've been in each other's company better than a third of my life. It has been a time of unparalleled happiness and spiritual growth, made all the richer because we have been able to share it with thousands of people in person and millions more thanks to our book publishers and to people like Oprah Winfrey and Leeza Gibbons.

It took me a long time to come to appreciate the transformative power of relationships. In high school I had to write an essay on something I believed in. I still have it. The first line says, "There are very few things I know for certain, but one thing I know for certain is that I will never, ever get married." Freedom was the issue, although I don't think I could have articulated it at the time. I very much wanted to carry out my own dreams and visions, and I felt that to commit myself to another person would block my freedom to do that. What I saw around me reinforced this rigid position. Married people seemed to be in a trance.

Now I have turned my view upside down (or right side up, to be more accurate). Not only do I feel that it is possible to stay awake and be in a long-term relationship, I believe that close relationships are our primary means of awakening. I believe now that relationship itself is the ultimate spiritual path, not simply an outcome of spiritual practice. If we cannot learn how to be free and be in close relationship at the same time, we cannot learn to be free. That is why conscious relationship is a required course, one that continues throughout life.

Let me give you an example of a lesson from the lifelong course. Using videoconferencing technology, I often counsel couples and individuals in faraway places. The technology works just fine and actually has one distinct advantage over being together in person. Due to a slight lag time, the machinery gets confused when people on either end try to speak at once. It rewards listening until the other person has stopped speaking before replying. Would that human beings came equipped with such a device from birth!

A married couple, both fifty, sat in a comfortable room in Texas, and I sat in a similar room in Santa Barbara. After a few minutes of getting reacquainted, I invited them to tell me and each other what they wanted to work on. Her complaint was that he traveled too much. His complaint was that she didn't support his spiritual practices. According to him, she criticized him subtly for taking time to meditate. She also was not being supportive of a trip he had planned to Asia.

I asked them several key questions to start the healing process. I have found that if I ask these questions up front, the therapy process takes much less time. The first two questions establish the purpose of the session:

Do you both want to be here?

Are you willing to solve the problems you've brought?

The first question is important, because many people come into counseling—especially couples' counseling—to please the other person or because they feel under pressure to come. In other words, one person may have chosen to come, while the other person feels compelled. This attitude must be handled at the outset to avoid wasted time and sabotaged plans later on.

The second question is important because many people come to counseling with hidden agendas. They are there not to solve their problems but to make the other person wrong, to get agreement from the therapist that the other person is bad, or to justify a decision they have already made. These intentions must be clarified and owned at once, lest the therapist become an unwitting ally in meeting these subterranean needs.

They answered yes to both of the questions, as I suspected they would, because they had been through the process before. Then I asked two further questions:

Are you both willing to tell the unarguable truth about the issues you bring?

Are you both willing to take full responsibility for creating the issues you bring?

Again, because they had worked with me before, they answered yes. I can assure you, though, that it doesn't always work quite so easily. Often the latter question inspires a flurry of resistance. Responsibility is not only essential to the counseling process, it also gets to the heart of metaphysics. Do we feel connected with our source in the universe? Or do we feel that we are the victim of any aspect of it? These are crucial questions we all must answer; in counseling they become highly practical keys to the healing process.

When I had secured their yes to these questions, I invited them to stand facing each other.

"Complete the following sentence to each other," I said. To Tim, I gave this sentence:

I require lack of support for my spirituality because ______________________________.

I gave this sentence to Josie:

I require long periods of time with Tim gone because ______________________________.

Many people argue with taking this much responsibility. I did, too, at an earlier stage of my maturity. Soon, though, we realize that the only hope of genuine growth comes from taking responsibility for everything we have previously claimed victimhood for. I don't mean that you have to go back into the past to take responsibility. True responsibility—the kind that changes your life—begins right now, the moment you take it. Most likely you didn't invite your drunken father to come home and beat you up when you were three, so there is no need to take responsibility for it. Take responsibility right now for the situations in your life that are replays of the original situation.

It took me a long time to figure out something I now know deep in my cells: we create the very situations we complain about most. Our unconscious programming causes us to pick certain people to play out our dramas with us, then when they do so we criticize them for it. Before I met Kathlyn, I unconsciously selected women who did not tell the truth and take responsibility. It was totally just and appropriate that I would do so, because I did not tell the truth and I was completely convinced I was the victim. My mother was the most critical person I have ever met, so it is natural I would select women who were intensely critical. Then, after going to the trouble of picking them (unconsciously, of course) I would complain about their being critical! The day I woke up to how life actually worked, those relationships ended. Fortunately, I got the message and invited Kathlyn into my life. Now years can go by without either of us criticizing the other.

Josie and Tim, on the other end of the video hookup, were about to enter the zone of the unknown. An old saying in therapy circles is "You're never upset for the reason you think you are." We may think we're upset because our partner doesn't support our spirituality or because our partner travels so much, but that's in the zone of the known. Problems don't get solved in that zone. They only get solved by revealing that which has lain hidden from us.

When Tim first said his sentence, nothing came out his mouth to fill in the blank. I invited him to keep saying the sentence over and over, to prime the pump of his unconscious mind. Finally, he gained access to a stream of awareness.

"I create lack of support for my spirituality because I don't feel I deserve to be here at all."

"I create lack of support for my spirituality because I . . ."

As he said this he gasped slightly and felt the early symptoms of an asthma attack (asthma has been a challenge for him since he was a little boy). I have worked with hundreds of asthmatics, so I had a reasonably sure grasp of what needed to happen next.

I invited him to notice where his breathing was centered—shallow and high in his chest—and to drop its center down into his lower belly.

"Take slow, deep, belly breaths," I said, "and pay attention to the emotions in your body."

"I feel a heaviness in my chest," he said.

"That sounds like sadness," I said, "but check it out in yourself and see if that's what it feels like to you."

He tuned in to it, and as he focused his attention on the emotion his breathing became fine again.

"Yeah, I'm sad and it's just like being in the oxygen tent with nobody around when I was a kid." As we talked about this event, I discovered that he not only had spent lonely times in the oxygen tent, but also that these times were his earliest spiritual moments as well. Perhaps it was being near death, or perhaps it was being flooded with pure oxygen, but he had a number of exalted spiritual feelings during these trips to the hospital. He came to dread them and to look forward to them at the same time.

Here was the source of his program, the very place where he decided, "I can't be supported for my spirituality." Our unconscious minds seem to take snapshots of reality moments like this. This leads us to take an unconscious position that life must be a certain way. Then, of course, life becomes that way. Now we shifted to Josie. As she repeated her sentence, she was flooded with an understanding of why she might tend to create a life with a husband gone much of the time. Her father had died at an early age, and the context in which she had grown up was that "men are never there for you." The women in her family were strong and self-sufficient and could make do just fine without men, thank you very much. That was her snapshot of how life had to be.

The feeling of tenseness between Tim and Josie dissolved immediately. I could see the change come over them even though I was watching them on television two thousand miles away. They leaned closer together, and smiles broke out on their faces. We had done the essential work of the session, and now they could work as allies again.

I want to reemphasize that they got these awarenesses right away because they were willing to tell the truth and take healthy responsibility for the issues they faced. That's why I make a practice of asking people up front whether they are willing to tell the truth and take responsibility. We begin with these conscious commitments, and then if clients wander from them I can stop them in mid-drama and ask them to honor their commitments again. Before I caught on to the power of commitment, I had seen it take months to unwind similar problems.

This example shows why relationships can be so difficult. A marital issue at fifty can be connected to sitting in an oxygen tent as a kid! That's why it takes such a powerful commitment to learning in order to steer through the rocky places in relationship.

Conscious Sex

One would think that sex would be easy to talk about, particularly in this age of talk shows, self-help books, and sex education courses. It is not. My wife and I have worked with hundreds of couples and individuals to help resolve their sexual issues. Over the years we have worked with probably every sexual difficulty with which people struggle. In addition, we have put energy into making our own sexual relationship rich and fulfilling. Out of all these experiences, we have developed strong convictions about sexuality in relationships.

Here are two of the most important ones.

1. Sexual problems are seldom about sex. Sex is the canary in the coal mine. When the canary keels over, coal miners do not apply CPR to the bird. They focus on fixing the larger problem, often invisible and pervasive, that is behind the obvious and visible bird problem. In over 90 percent of the cases in which I have been con-

sulted regarding sexual problems, the sexual issues cleared up when more fundamental problems were handled. About 10 percent of the time, there was actually something wrong with the physiology or the technical aspects of sex that needed addressing.

Sexual communication is the solution to almost every sexual problem. Again, amazingly enough, we receive little or no training in this crucial life skill in the traditional educational system. We have to learn it by trial and error, emphasis on the error. Some of the most awkward moments of my life have been in the area of sexual communication, and I have certainly witnessed hundreds more such moments in therapy. The voice box is the most important sexual organ we have and the one we need to pay closest attention to. We will explore this area in more detail later.

2. A second major learning about sex is this: monogamy is the only path I've ever seen that works. My sexual relationships began in the sixties, a time of great sexual freedom. I experimented with so-called open relationships, in which both people were able to have other sexual partners. I tried having multiple partners without telling them about one another, then I went to the opposite extreme of telling the scrupulous truth to all concerned. I very much wanted to have sexual freedom in my relationships. By nature I am an adventurer and a connoisseur of new experiences, and I dislike being tied down to a limited set of experiences and expectations. Remember, I was the guy who said he would never, ever get married.

In spite of all this, by the time I met Kathlyn I had become a convert to monogamy. The main reason was practical: everything else was chaotic and required so much processing time! It was almost impossible to stay in integrity with all parties concerned. It seemed to take all our time and energy dealing with the wounded feelings all around. There was little energy left over for creativity and good times. Plus, jealousy feels awful to me, and I found I was more consumed by this feeling than I cared to admit.

Nowadays, of course, having multiple sexual partners is not merely complicated but potentially lethal. This was an issue that did not enter into many conversations in the sixties and seventies but is in the background of all of them today. All in all, I am grateful I had the opportunity to experiment and doubly grateful that I learned that monogamy is the only path for me. Setting aside all other reasons I have mentioned, monogamy offers one compelling advantage: if I commit myself totally to one partner, I create the momentum necessary to bring all my issues to the surface and potentially clear them up. If I do not commit to one partner, I slow the momentum and fritter away the evolutionary potential of the relationship.

Many people have stood up in lectures and taken issue with me on this subject. They have argued against monogamy and extolled the virtue of other paradigms. I always ask these people if they personally know examples of creative, long-term relationships in which people have multiple sexual partners. To date, no one has told me about anything that works.

The Possibilities of Conscious Sex

Sex is fraught with problems for many of us, but it also offers us the most potent field for transformation. When you go inside the body of another person or vice versa, you set in motion forces that carry the seeds both of creation and destruction. Our physical bodies are in play during sex. However, this is only the smallest part of why sex plays such a role in transformation. I predict that when science develops more sophisticated machinery for measuring our energy bodies and even our spiritual essence, we'll find that these parts of us are much more sensitive than we ever dreamed.

The rich interplay of physical sensation during sex is probably vastly overshadowed by the symphony of activity in the subtle bodies of our energy network and our spiritual essence. These subtle bodies will likely be discovered to extend beyond the boundaries of the physical body. It certainly feels that way to me. When I tune in carefully to myself, I notice subtle fluctuations inside me that occur when people draw near, even if they do not touch me physically. That is why the transformative potential of sex does not require physical contact, but if there is actual physical contact the guarantee of transformation is absolute.

Sex fuels transformation because it pulls more than sexual sensation to the surface. It brings up undealt-with material from prior times in your life when others were inside your boundaries. It doesn't matter whether you invited them there or they forced their way in—it's really all the same. There were times when others were inside our boundaries, and there were times when we felt wounded by the experience in some way. When we open our boundaries to another person now, the act of doing so brings our archaic issues to the surface. That is why only a sexual relationship is likely to provide the ultimate fuel for transformation.

I have worked in therapy with dozens of people who were in celibate religious vocations before deciding to enter the world of sexual relationships. All of them told me a similar story, and it fits with my own experience. They did not gain access to the deepest level of their defenses and their programming until they made a sexual commitment. These deeper issues simply did not come up when they were celibate. By allowing their defenses to surface, they gained the opportunity to move through them and experience greater joy than before. In my own relationships, I notice that the act of making a commitment brings up the deepest issues. And certainly sexual commitment brings them up most quickly. By focusing your sexual energy on one person, you bring up material from the times in your life when your survival depended on people who were inside the boundaries of your body.

We were conceived and gestated within the boundaries of another person's body. Then, after we were born, the majority of us took another person's body inside ours every day. During nursing, we not only have another person's body inside ours, but our very survival is at stake. It is only natural that later in life, when we open our boundaries to another, deep survival issues are brought to the fore.

The Strongest Aphrodisiac

Truthful words, spoken with good intention, are the most powerful aphrodisiac of all. We lose sexual interest in people to whom we lie. A subtle hidden feeling, such as swallowed anger or hurt, can cast an instant pall over sexual feeling. A bigger lie, such as sexual attraction or sexual activity with another person, can turn off the flow of sexual energy. If we are to have healthy sexuality, it is paramount that we speak the transparent truth of all our feelings to the significant person in our lives.

Sexuality thrives in a rich field of expressed feeling. Feeling is feeling, whether it is "I felt hurt when you said . . ." or "I felt a rush of joy when I saw how beautiful you look in that dress." As long as we are speaking from the truth of our emotional experience, we are contributing to a healthy sexual environment as well as a healthy environment in general.

In working with hundreds of sexual issues in therapy, I have learned something that I also practice in my own sexual relationship: telling the truth is the most potent healer of sexual problems. I cannot overemphasize this point. My files are full of miracles that happened just after a withheld truth was revealed. My own life is testament to this also. Many times I have felt my sexual feelings wane, only to return strongly when I told the truth about something I was withholding.

If your partner looks boring to you, it is usually because you are holding some lie. If your sexual life is unfulfilled in some way, it is usually because there is some truth you need to tell. This may sound harsh and radical, but I mean it kindly. I would want you to tell me this if you knew it and I didn't. Once you taste the power of what I'm describing, I predict you will develop a deep respect for the power of truth to heal your life.

The Intention That Creates Sexual Fulfillment

Mixed intention is another fundamental issue that can destroy sexual communication. This needs to be said loudly and clearly: the intention behind your sexual energy is crucial. Think of sexual energy as a beam directed toward someone, who in turn beams sexual energy at you. If there are mixed intentions about sexuality, crosswise energy currents are set in motion that create problems for all participants. Some intentions enhance the beam and make it clear and strong. Other intentions, what I am calling crosscurrents, interfere with the beam and make sexuality a source of problems.

There is only one intention that brings ultimate sexual fulfillment: to celebrate the essence of your partner and yourself through your lovemaking. Nothing else works. Since we live in a culture where sex is used to sell everything from tobacco to toothpaste, it is not surprising that our intentions are often mixed with regard to sex. We become brainwashed to think sex is to get something, not to celebrate something. We learn to use sex as a manipulation, a means toward some other end. It takes a great deal of commitment to return to the essence of what sex is really for.

There is another hidden intention behind much of the sexuality that goes on in the world. Sex is used as a salve for other feelings, such as loneliness. We grow lonely and confused, and we reach for another person to blunt the pain, just as we might reach for the liquor bottle or the cookie bag. Sex has medicinal properties, and since our largest sex organ is our skin, it is easy to dull the pain of our isolation with doses of sex.

To get your intentions clear, begin with a commitment: "I commit to having all my sexual experiences celebrate my partner's essence and my own." If this is something you really want, your commitment will begin to spread through you and affect your actions. When I was an adolescent, I thought only of my own sexual gratification. When I fantasized about girls as a pubescent male, I definitely was not thinking of their essence. Even when I began having full-scale sexual relationships in my later teen years, I didn't give any thought to celebrating my own essence or my partner's. It took me into my late twenties to learn that sex is a dance of spirit that is not based on physical friction at all.

Eight Sexual Conversations

Since 90 percent of our problems with sexuality are related to communication, we need to take a detailed look at what kinds of communication can solve those problems. The solutions are remarkably simple, though it has taken me half my life to learn to practice them skillfully.

I have made a point of asking clients and professionals in training what they wish they had learned about sex and sexual communication. What do we most need to learn about sexual communication?

What learnings could make our lives easier and more fulfilled? What could help us prevent the awesome pain caused by sexual confusion and difficulty? What could enhance our enjoyment of sexuality? I have asked these questions many times with hundreds of people from ten years of age to past seventy, and I have carefully recorded their answers.

The learnings fall into eight main areas—some practical and technical, some metaphorical, but all highly charged. I will describe these areas, then present a single communication technique that has emerged over the years as the most powerful method of communicating about sexual issues.

1. Saying What You Need

Saying what you need in sexually charged moments is the number one learning people have said they needed. A woman at one of our trainings gave an extreme illustration of the problem. She told us she had given birth to four children before she was eighteen. She said two of the children were born before anyone told her how girls got pregnant. Two more were born because she didn't know a way to say, "Don't ejaculate inside me." Like many of us, she came from a culture where neither women nor men were given the information they needed to make life-changing decisions about sex. Even in my mother's lifetime, people went to jail in the U.S. for disseminating information about contraception. In addition, the woman told us that in her culture, women "just didn't say those kinds of things." Women were supposed to defer to the needs of men, and this is the way it is in much of the world. Finally she learned to speak up about her needs and did not get pregnant again for ten years, even though she used no mechanical form of contraception.

Saying what you need is the most important aspect of sexual communication. What you need is the one thing, the bottom line, the crucial issue that must be addressed to make your sexual fulfillment possible.

- I need you to use a condom.
- I need you to know I was once raped and sometimes freeze up.
- I need to be absolutely certain I won't get pregnant.

It is important not to confuse need and want. Need usually refers to one thing and is a requirement. Don't say "I need . . ." unless you are referring to something that must happen. Need usually addresses a fear, and speaking your need is designed to ease that fear. Different from saying what you need, saying what you want is designed to maximize positive potential. It is essential that we know what our needs are—to be clear about them and not to rely on telepathy from our partners to guess them—so that we can open the door to the possibility of fulfillment.

2. Saying What You Want

Saying what you want is the second key learning in sexuality. Saying what you want expresses a preference.

- I want you to touch me like this . . .
- I want to talk to you about something before we make love.
- I want you to put the lights on softly.

Learning to say what you want opens a possibility for the full flowering of your sexuality. For full flowering to take place, we must be in deep harmony with our wants, and we must be able to tell others what they are. Telling someone what you like sexually is an art that is not easy to learn. I found it difficult because of the fear of rejection. Sexual requests are often made in moments of vulnerability when the pain of rejection is amplified. Once in a moment of vulnerability I told a partner that I wanted her to touch me in a certain way. She looked mildly pained, which my perception amplified into disgust. I felt my stomach sink, my groin tighten. The spirit of the moment was tainted, and I felt myself draw back into a sullen pout.

"What's wrong?" she asked. But I couldn't tell her. I had pulled back into myself, and in those days I did not know how to get back out. There I stayed, while the minutes turned into hours. Finally, when I was able to tell her what happened, she told me that my request had reminded her of a painful moment in her life. It had nothing to do with me, but she didn't know how to tell me about it, either. This leads us to the third difficult area of sexual communication.

3. Talking About Emotional Issues Related to Sex

Often the deepest human feelings emerge from ourselves before, during, and after sex. Unless we know how to communicate about them, we are lost. Usually what happens is that sexual activity will flush to the surface some archaic painful issue that is unresolved. For example, one of my clients had the following experience. She met a man she liked and had dinner with him several times. Things progressed, and she invited him into her bedroom one evening, where they both undressed and got under the covers. The last thing he did before slipping beneath the covers was to place his glasses on the bedside table. At this she began to hyperventilate, an experience that had never occurred to her before. She said later that it was as if she had separated from her body and was watching it "do this strange breathing thing." Her new friend pulled back, stunned and confused, and asked what was wrong. "Nothing's wrong," she screamed, then passed out. When she awoke a few minutes later, he had called 911 and the emergency squad was on the way.

As she dissected what she called her "date from hell," we tracked down the archaic issue that had been triggered. When she was thirteen, an uncle had come to stay with her family when he was discharged from the service. He molested her several times before she blew the whistle on him. Her father threw him out, and the incident was never mentioned again. The trigger was this: when the uncle would come into her room to fondle her, he would put his glasses down on her bedside table. Years later, even with a man she liked, this simple act threw her physiology into terror. After we uncovered this old wound, we invited her new boyfriend in for a session in which we discussed the occurrence in the light of this new information. They talked it through—even having a good, cathartic laugh about it—and grew closer as a result.

This sort of occurrence is rare, but subtle versions of it go on in the bedroom all the time. An emotion is triggered by some sexual event, and this emotion comes to the fore. One second we're feeling sexy, and the next moment we shut down or flare up. What do we do in such situations? Do we communicate about it or let it go? We need to know how to communicate in the moments before, during, and after sex when unexpected feelings course through our bodies.

What happens is that the energy of sex stirs to the surface something that was "bubbling under," whether it was from this morning or thirty years ago. No one knows why issues come to the surface when they do. Rarely are we able to spot a specific trigger, such as my client did in the example above. But issues do arise, and the same principle applies to mundane emotional communications as to the deeper types of trauma described in the date from hell. "I was irritated today when you forgot to buy detergent" is as likely to cause wrinkles in the bed as a more dramatic trauma.

Many people have told me that the hardest thing for them in sexual communication is talking about the little niggling things that seem too trivial to bring up. They don't bring them up, and invariably their sexual experience is dampened as a result. Others have told me that their most difficult moment in sexual communication is their confusion about whether or not what they're doing is working. Many people get anxious that they are not pleasing their partners, and they don't know how to get feedback or to communicate their lack of ease.

I recommend a radically simple treatment when issues and feelings emerge in lovemaking. Go ahead and talk about them on the spot. Do not put them aside until later. Say something about them, using the tried-and-true communication technique I'll show you later. You will likely find, as hundreds of others have, that you do not have to do this very often. As soon as your body learns that it is all right for emotional issues to surface during sex—and that you have a way to handle them—it will often stop sending these signals at those times. It is actually possible to ask your body not to release archaic emotions during sex, once your body understands that you are willing to deal with these feelings at some point. In other words, once we let go of our stance of denial—befriending our bodies and listening to them—we are able to enter a dialogue with them as equals.

4. Initiating Sex

How to begin? How to make the transition from the social realm to the sexual? These are questions many of us will encounter throughout our lives. When sex is going well, there is an organic and smooth transition of talk and touch to the deeper engagement of sexual intercourse. I can remember such times—they seem graced and full of light—but they have not happened for me even a majority of the time. Often the transition to sex has been accompanied by hesitation, stutter, and clumsiness that probably could have been prevented if I'd known how to talk about what I was feeling.

The breakthrough for me came in the midseventies when I was first beginning to catch on to the power of truth telling. Picking up the phone to call a woman I'd met recently, I noticed that I felt nervous. I had probably felt nervous in many such situations in the past, but for some reason this time I noticed the precise qualities of it. I could feel butterfly sensations in my stomach, along with a dryness in my mouth. As I was feeling all this, she picked up the phone and said "Hello."

I identified myself and said, "I'm nervously calling to ask you to go out with me."

There was a pause, then a chuckle.

"I appreciate your honesty," she said. "I nervously accept."

I remember this conversation as a watershed point in my ability to communicate with people. Suddenly I realized I could simply say what I was feeling, and the worst that could happen was that they could have some reaction to it. But their reaction was none of my business. In other words, I didn't need to edit the authenticity of any of my communications out of fear of their reactions. I had no control over how they reacted. I could put all my attention on knowing the truth and speaking it in a straightforward way.

5. Talking About Sexual Rejection

Sexual rejection is the hardest thing to speak about for many of us. Social rejection feels bad enough, but sexual rejection is beyond bad. Most people tell me that they feel sexual rejection at a place deeper in the body than social rejection. I have asked many people over the years to tell me where they feel the pain of social rejection, and most of them will touch their chests, usually on the left side. However, when I ask where they feel the pain of sexual rejection, they will usually touch their lower abdomen, in the pelvis or near the hip joints. Sexual rejection probably affects us more at the core because it is related to the life-or-death issue of regeneration.

6. Talking About Sexual Fantasies

"What do I do," a good friend asks me as we walk along the beach together, "when I'm making love with my wife but fantasizing about my secretary? I'm trying to be completely honest in my marriage, but wouldn't telling her about my fantasy be going a little too far?" This sums up a dilemma that many of us need to face. Like you, I have awakened to the incredible power of authenticity in my close relationships. The more truthful I get, the better they work. When I hide the truth, my relationships quickly turn into entanglements. But how far do I go?

The answer is absolutely simple: tell the absolute truth about everything in any relationship in which you want absolute intimacy. Withhold and edit where you are not so sure. If your desire is for absolute intimacy, risk it all by speaking of everything. If your intention is clear—the intention to produce intimacy—you cannot produce any other result. If your intention is mixed—for example, if you are telling the truth to wound the other person—you will likely produce a mixed result. Truths told for any reason other than to produce intimacy quickly backfire on the teller.

Here is a list of fantasies that people have told their partners, with no damage at all to the relationship.

- Making love to the partner's sibling
- Making love to the partner's best friend
- Group sex
- Bondage and other sex games

In other words, I have seen even those communications add strength and harmony to close relationships. However, they need to be communicated in a certain way. At the end of this section, we will explore a way of communicating about sensitive sexual material, a way that produces harmony reliably.

7. Talking About Sexual Difficulties

Many of us have trouble talking about problems that we are experiencing in our sexual relationships. While it is often difficult to talk about sexual difficulties with anyone, it seems especially hard to talk about them with the most significant other person. As a film buff, I have seen dozens of movies in which a man has failed to get an erection. It is almost always depicted with the man looking dejected, chin down on chest, with the woman propped on her elbow reassuring him that it's all right. Why is it that the moment itself is never depicted? Where is the sparkling dialogue that would tell us what to say in those situations?

I have never seen a film with the female perspective illustrated. For example, I have yet to see a movie in which a woman experiences failure to achieve an orgasm. Her chin would be slumped on her chest, and the man would be propped on his elbow, reassuring her that she was all right. Is this a testament to the pervasive sexism in the world, or is it simply because most movies are written and directed by men? If there were such a film, what would the characters be saying to each other?

That dialogue has yet to be invented, because we are just now learning what kind of communication works in such sensitive situations.

8. Communicating with the Sexual Energy Inside Us

A final issue of sexual communication is not really about the spoken word at all. It is our relationship with the sexual energy we feel inside us. In a way, however, it is the most important communication of all. Sexual energy is life energy itself. There really is no difference between sexual energy and all the humming activity of our trillions of cells, because all of it came from an explosion of sexual creation. By the same token, the streaming vibrancy of our entire being had its source in sexual union. It's our "always, everywhere" state of being; it's in us and we're in it.

The message is clear: how we are with our sexual energy is how we are—period. Having said this, the question arises, "What is the best sort of relationship to have with sexual energy?" From my therapy experience, the only relationship I've seen that works is to think of your sexual energy as your best friend. When I think of my closest friend (who has been my best friend for twenty-five years), I think of the following qualities our relationship has:

- When we're together, I enjoy the time immensely.
- I give my full attention to the relationship when we're together.
- I rely on the relationship for counsel.
- I feel absolute equals in the relationship.
- We don't have any rigid expectations of each other. For example, our respective wives have never spent a minute alone with each other, and the four of us almost never get together.

- When we're together, we are open to spontaneity. I can't remember planning an activity in the past twenty-five years. We may go for a walk on the beach, to a restaurant for lunch, onto the squash court for an hour of high-test(osterone) competition, or we may simply linger over an espresso while we catch up.

These are all qualities that are useful to have with your sexual energy. To be specific:

- Let go of expectations of your sexuality. Sexual energy is like the weather—highly changeable, hard to predict, and running the range of intensity from typhoon strength to gentle breeze. It's always there, in the background of everything, even when it's not doing much that you would notice.
- Put your attention on enjoying sexual energy, not controlling it. Celebrate it while it's there, and look for ways to contribute to others' enjoying it, too.
- Think of your sexuality as an equal. Some people have a master-slave relationship with their sexuality. One group thinks sex is their boss—it's bigger than they are and orders them around—while others think they are the boss and they can order their sexuality around. Both are wrong. Since we are our sexuality, we are absolute equals with it. It could not be otherwise. It's all in how you think of it. If you think you are equals with your sexuality, you are. Even if you don't think you are, you still are, but your chances of enjoying yourself are radically diminished.
- If you think of your sexuality as your equal, you can rely on it for advice and counsel. As a guide to life decisions, your sexual energy is astute. For example, I worked with a couple

> who enjoyed their sexual energy and lovemaking a lot. They had other issues to contend with, but sex wasn't one of them. Because they were so in touch with their sexual energy, we were able to use it to help them make a decision.
>
> They had a major choice to make involving a career move to the Mideast for several years. To help them make the decision, I invited them to tune in to their sexual energy and find out if it increased or decreased when they thought of moving to the Mideast. At first they thought this an odd thing to do, but right away they noticed that both of them felt an increased sexual buzz when they thought about moving. This information, combined with logical considerations, helped them make their move.

As you grow more comfortable with these important conversations, you will find that you have more access to sexual energy. In fact, most of my students and clients report that they have a great deal more sexual energy than they could possibly act on. What can we do with all this excess?

The Use of Sexual Energy for Manifestation

There is no question that human beings are endowed with a great deal more sexual energy than we can possibly use. It is to evolution's advantage to set it up this way. Women are born with hundreds of eggs, most or all of which will go unfertilized. Men could potentially father more than a million children a day, providing all the sperm we manufacture find an egg. Many of us have many more fantasy sexual experiences than we could possibly keep track of in real life.

Sexual energy is abundant, but how we express it must be finite and circumscribed. The question becomes: what creative use could we put all that energy to? How could we take advantage of this surplus of sexuality? The answer: to fuel our life goals. If we know how to channel sexual energy, we can draw on this vast storehouse of energy to energize our creativity.

I came across this odd idea in an equally odd way. In therapy, I saw any number of people who were troubled by excess sexual energy. Some of these identified themselves as sex addicts, while others labeled themselves as obsessive fantasizers. Looking beneath the surface of these issues, it became clear that sexual thoughts, flirtations, and dramas were being used by them as a way of blocking their creativity. These people were often wildly creative, but they had channeled their creativity into one limited mode of expression. When these clients got better, it was almost always because they found and nurtured alternative pathways to express their creative/sexual energies.

These experiences led us to theorize that the excess sexual energy we produce has more than one evolutionary purpose. It is certainly for procreation, but it can also be used for creativity itself. I cannot begin to tell you the amount of relief that people have experienced when they found that they did not have to block their sexual energy but merely redirect it.

In the final chapter of the book, we will explore how to direct this energy into manifesting specific projects.

Sexual Enhancement

With regard to sexual enhancement, Kathlyn and I have developed three techniques that have proved successful in deepening enjoyment during sex. They are: paying close attention to breathing patterns; communicating in a new way; and touching for sexual enhancement.

The Breathing Patterns of Sexual Fulfillment

Imagine that you are sexually interested in someone. You touch the person, perhaps a sensual touch on the forearm, and something about the person's reaction inspires you to continue. Chances are, you have subliminally observed a change in the person's breathing pattern. There is a breathing pattern that lets you know the person is sexually receptive, and there is one that signals "stop right there." We need to know these signals so that we can be in the stream of sexual energy more easily. Let's begin at the beginning.

In the beginning of a sexual encounter with a willing partner, the first type of breathing to emerge is flowing breath. It is longer and deeper than ordinary breathing. If people are interested in you sexually, their breathing will deepen as you move closer to them. If not, you will see ragged or hesitant breathing patterns. A complicating factor here is that often people are interested and afraid at the same time because of past traumas or inhibiting messages about sex. In such situations, however, the ragged or hesitant pattern must still be addressed. If you try to override it, it will come back to haunt you later. Furthermore, at any point along the way, a hesitant or ragged breath may appear, signaling that fear has entered the process. It is common for sexual arousal to flush to the surface fear patterns from earlier in life, situations that often have nothing specifically to do with sex. For instance, birth trauma can cause inhibitions in breathing that show up later during sexual arousal.

For the purposes of our discussion, I will describe the four remaining breathing patterns that are organic to sexual arousal. We will assume that a smooth progression takes place from initial arousal through climax, with no glitches occurring along the way.

As sensation builds, the flowing breath is replaced by a shorter, sharper breath that has more defined beginnings and endings.

While the flowing breath is long and deep and melts from in-breath to out-breath, the pumping breath is quick and staccato. As sexual energy builds toward climax, the pumping breath dissolves into a mixed pattern in which the length of each breath varies from breath to breath. Generally quite rapid, it is a spontaneous breathing pattern, in which the out-breath may begin before the in-breath is finished and vice versa. This pattern continues through orgasm, following which a fourth pattern takes over.

The streaming pattern is lighter and often longer than the flowing pattern, which it resembles. It is frequently accompanied by an open-ended or liquid sound on the out-breath (for example, aaaaaaa or mmmmm). After a cool-down period, the streaming pattern slows to the quiet pattern, which is often so light that the person appears not to be breathing at all. I observe this same quiet pattern in deep meditation, when the person is awake yet very still.

By knowing these breathing patterns we can appreciate them, relax into them, and enhance our enjoyment of sexuality. Knowing the breath more intimately also allows us to spot the ragged or hesitant patterns that let us know we're scared about something. Many cases of sexual dysfunction can be spotted and treated by observing which of the five breathing patterns the person cannot carry through to completion. By knowing the five patterns, the person can practice them a few minutes a day as a self-help technique. They can be done by oneself or with a partner. If the person gives a few weeks to practicing them, there will nearly always be a noticeable enhancement of sexual enjoyment. Sometimes I have seen seemingly miraculous healings. For example, a woman who had lost her hearing after a sexual trauma regained both her hearing and her sexual feelings after a session of attention to the breathing patterns.

Super-Resonance: A New Way of Communicating

Kathlyn and I have spent many years working with a new way of communicating before, during, and after sex. We call it super-resonance. In super-resonant communication, you say things that resonate with your own deepest self. When this occurs, it stimulates resonance in the deepest self of your partner. The goal is to speak in such a way that you are communicating about the actual resonances you are feeling in your body. When you connect with this level, you immediately stimulate the resonance of the other person. For example, you may be sitting next to your partner watching television. Your partner rubs his or her leg against yours in a way that feels good. A nonresonant communication would be to say, "Rub your leg against me like that more." This communication issues a command, and although they may be well intended, commands often produce negative results. The same message could be communicated in super-resonance by saying, "I'm feeling streams of delicious energy running up my body from the way your leg is rubbing against me." This communication expresses a very specific inner awareness. It simply reports something that is happening on a deep level. You are using your voice box to make sounds that correspond as exactly as possible to inner resonances. At first it takes practice; don't expect to be great at it the first time. However, it produces results even when applied unskillfully. If your intentions are good (a sincere desire to express yourself and enhance you and your partner's experience) you will find that the response is immediate and positive. Those who have tried it are invariably amazed at how quickly the other person responds.

Sometimes, learning super-resonance techniques brings about healing of deep sexual wounds with no other intervention. (An interesting side note: during workshops in which people are learning to communicate in this new way, the temperature in the room often goes up by five to ten degrees, even though most participants are not directly communicating about sex.)

Here are some super-resonant communications to illustrate their tone and flavor.

- I'm feeling a vibrating sensation in my thighs.
- As I look into your eyes, I feel a lightheadedness.
- My bloodstream feels like it's singing.
- My heart feels so open and happy.
- I feel these wonderful butterfly sensations deep in my belly.

If you are feeling something unpleasant, super-resonance will often help dissolve the block you're feeling.

- I feel a tightness in my belly, like a knot.
- I'm still wound up from work. My shoulders are bunched up, and I feel a pressure on my chest.

It usually does not take much super-resonant communication before the sensations begin to change. Sometimes, in fact, you'll notice them begin to shift as you're speaking about them.

An Experiential Interlude

The only way to appreciate super-resonance fully is to practice it. The following exercise is simple, yet I have seen it create astonishing results. If you have a partner, stand face-to-face and practice it with him or her. If you don't have anyone to practice with, stand facing a full-length mirror.

Person A will describe the sensations in a particular area of the body. The communication should be as specific as you can make it, and it should take no longer than one out-breath. Do your best not to say anything arguable (for example, "I'm feeling a lump in my throat, and it's all your fault"). Person B will then repeat back exactly what you heard, with no interpretation or spin.

Here is an example:

PERSON A: In my throat I am feeling a lumpy, clogged sensation.
PERSON B: In your throat you're feeling a lumpy, clogged sensation.

Each part of the body will be the focus of three communication interchanges. In other words, the example above would continue:

PERSON A: In my throat I am feeling a pleasant feeling of relaxation beginning.
PERSON B: In your throat you're feeling a pleasant feeling of relaxation beginning.
PERSON A: In my throat I'm feeling a melting sensation.
PERSON B: In your throat you're feeling a melting sensation.

The exercise begins with the throat and works through other parts of the body, with three communications per part. After one person gets all the way through, it's the other person's turn.

- In my throat I feel . . .
- In my throat I feel . . .
- In my throat I feel . . .

- In my chest I feel . . .
- In my chest I feel . . .
- In my chest I feel . . .

- In my belly I feel . . .
- In my belly I feel . . .
- In my belly I feel . . .

- In my pelvis I feel . . .
- In my pelvis I feel . . .
- In my pelvis I feel . . .

- In my legs I feel . . .
- In my legs I feel . . .
- In my legs I feel . . .

- In my arms I feel . . .
- In my arms I feel . . .
- In my arms I feel . . .

- In my back I feel . . .
- In my back I feel . . .
- In my back I feel . . .

Super-resonance is ideal for enhancing sexual pleasure, because it gives your partner precise information about your inner world. This in itself is erotic. Many of my clients have told me that they cannot get sexually turned on unless there is a deep level of communication, and I would echo this from my own experience. Kathlyn and I sometimes go through periods in which we seem to lose sexual interest in each other for a few days. Invariably, super-resonance is what brings it back. Eventually I will notice that I haven't been finding her sexually attractive, for example, and I'll remember to speak in super-resonance. "I feel some prickles of irritation in my arms," I might say, opening a gateway to super-resonant communication. "I've been feeling a held-back feeling in me, like I'm trying to control something." "Ah," I'll realize, "I'm angry about the situation between you and Nancy," referring to some work-related problem. I'll tell her more about it, giving as much detail as I can. Sometimes I will feel a return of sexual excitement just by communicating one small element of what's going on in me. The more we communicate in super-resonance, the stronger the flow of sexual energy becomes.

A New Way of Touching for Sexual Enhancement

Kathlyn and I made a fascinating and transformative discovery about ten years ago: when any two places on the body are touched at the same time in a specific way, both the toucher and the receiver go into an altered state of consciousness. We call this type of contact super-resonant touch. Although we originally made the discovery while doing body-centered therapy, it did not take us long to apply it to enhancing sexual pleasure. Now, we have developed a way of teaching people how to make the super-resonant level of contact. People at our workshops love it (it can be learned fully clothed as easily as in intimate environments).

You can try it right now. If you take a moment to notice your fingertips sensitively, you will find that there is a fine vibration going on beneath the surface of them. Focus your attention on the fingertips and pads of your fingers, inside the skin. It may take a moment to feel it, but I haven't found anyone yet who couldn't feel it. If it's not readily apparent, rub your fingertips and pads briskly together for about ten seconds to intensify the sensation. Once you have felt the subtle buzz of the vibration, select a finger that feels most sensitive. For me it is the index finger of my right hand that feels most sensitive.

Touch a place on your forearm with this finger. When you have made contact, feel the vibration of your finger, and also feel the vibration of the place you are touching on your forearm. This is super-resonant contact. Stay in touch with the super-resonance level of contact as you rub your forearm with your finger. If you lose connection with the vibration level of either place—finger or forearm—pause and reconnect.

Now you are ready to touch two places at once, which is the ultimate stage of super-resonant touch. When two places are touched at once, an altered state of consciousness is triggered that has very pleasant feelings. You'll see what I mean in a minor way on yourself and in a major way when you do it with a partner.

Select two fingers to do the touching. It works best if you use two fingers from different hands. The further apart the two places you touch are, the better results you'll get. Select a place to touch that you would like to make feel better.

Let me show you what I mean, using myself as an example. I used the middle fingers of each hand, and I picked my temples to touch. I wouldn't call the feeling in my temples a headache, but I can feel some pressure or tightness there that has been growing during the day. As I write this around nine in the evening, I am at the end of a full day, which included teaching a group of corporate executives, doing a therapy session with a prominent show business figure (with an equally prominent ego), and watching part of a World Series game in which my team lost. Perhaps like your day, mine had its ups and downs.

Closing my eyes, I rest the pads of each middle finger on my temples. I tune in to the vibration in my fingers and then feel the vibration of the temples. The vibration in my fingertips is subtle and fine, compared to the dull and leaden feel of my temples. As I meet vibration with vibration, though, a pleasant shift begins to occur. My eyes relax and seem to sink back in my head. I realize I had been straining somewhat all day so I could get done what needed to be done. Now I can feel my eyes softening, and as this happened the dull sensation shifts to a brighter feeling of ease. Suddenly I forget completely about my fingers, my temples, and what I am doing. A shift takes place in my mind, from slightly harried to pleasantly alert. I drift and float for ten or fifteen seconds, flowing with an inner wavelike sensation.

Then, like popping out of a pleasant trance, I remember where I am again. I become aware of my fingers and my temples, but now everything feels different. There is no more tension or gathered energy in my temples. In fact, there is little or no sensation at all, except a lightness and spaciousness.

This is super-resonance at work.

The Ultimate Potential of Conscious Sexuality

With the correct attitudes and skills, we can go through the gateway of conscious sex to tap a transcendental stream of energy that can heal as well as bring heightened pleasure. Even if the old trauma or pattern is not sexual in nature, the transcendental energy stream enables healing to take place. I have even seen physical injuries and maladies finally begin to heal when the person opens up a pathway to conscious sexuality. As yet I do not completely understand the mechanism by which this takes place, but it has occurred often enough that I no longer have doubts about it.

We all know about unconscious sex and unconscious relationships. Driven by our old programming, we do things we later regret and put ourselves into roles that are limited and often demeaning. Our old limitations cause us to settle for less than our relationships could be. Conscious relationship and its running mate, conscious sexuality, are new to us as human beings. We are just beginning to know enough about ourselves and our sexuality to tap its enormous potential for transformation.

I urge you to experiment with the principles and practices I have described. They have worked for thousands of people who were courageous enough to enter the zone of the unknown with regard to their relationships and their sexuality. Perhaps together we can create a transcendent form of love and sex that can leave a legacy of intimacy and spiritual growth to the lovers of the future.

CHAPTER 9

How to Create a Life of Your Own Design

The human brain is the most marvelous creation we know, and most of us are using only a tiny percentage of its power. It's as if we are given a jet airplane when we're born, but people tell us we can use it only to plow potato fields. It can fly—it wants to fly—but we taxi up and down the same bumpy rows every year, harvesting a meager ration of spuds.

We need to know that our programming can be changed, and we need to know how to do it. That brings us to the subject of manifestation, the art and science of creating life by your own design.

Manifestation is the art of choosing how you want your life to be and turning those choices into reality. Conscious manifestation begins the moment we stick our heads out from the fog layer of our programming and ask, "How would *I* like *my* life to be?"

Many of us never ask this question. Until we do, we merely want what we have been programmed to want. Until we ask that question, there is no freedom to innovate. The moment we ask it we join forces with the creative source of the universe; we go into partnership with life itself. That's why it's important to know how manifestation works. Without knowing the principles of manifestation, life is not a journey of discovery but an aimless ramble or a forced march.

For twenty-five years I've felt the joy of creating a life of my own design, and it's turned out better than I ever imagined. I'd like all humans to know the deep joys of creating a life that is informed but unfettered by the past.

A Question Kicked Off My Manifestation Journey

My first major breakthrough was initiated through the gift of a great question. When I was finishing up my doctorate at Stanford, I was asking deeply how I wanted to proceed in my career. Three people in the course of a week suggested I look up a maverick psychologist named Jim Fadiman who taught part-time at Stanford. Even though I had no idea why I wanted to talk to him, I called him up and walked over to his office. In our conversation, he asked me a question that would stay with me throughout my life: "What do you want?" Embedded in the question were several levels of meaning: How do you want your life to be? What contribution do you want to make? What is your special gift you can bring to the world?

His question was a shaft of light, and on my way back to my office I dreamed up my own future. By the time I reached my office I had planned a book for classroom teachers that could be used as a sourcebook for a new type of teaching. I called it *The Centering Book*, and I wrote it in a matter of weeks on a borrowed typewriter. I did my day job until 5 P.M., then often stayed up until 3 A.M. working on the book. I didn't miss the sleep, though, because I was so excited to be working in harmony with my own chosen purpose.

Up until then, writing had been something of a chore for me. Now it flowed easily because I was in the grip of the question: what do you most want? I was putting my heart and soul into the enterprise, not merely confirming but innovating. Not only did I write it effortlessly, but I immediately sold it to a major publisher and saw it become a best-seller in the educational market within the year.

We will return to this key question—What do I want?—when we explore the Twelve Laws of manifestation. Before we do, though, let's step back and look at the big picture. If you see how the principles of manifestation fit the way the universe works organically, you will be able to apply the techniques more readily.

Three Levels of Manifestation

The three levels of manifestation are similar to shifts the Western world has made in the understanding of physics. Level One techniques of manifestation—which I call "Newtonian" since they began to emerge after Newton set forth his laws of physics—are useful and powerful, and we need to understand them first, because they provide the foundation for the two advanced levels of manifestation.

Popular techniques like visualization or positive thinking are based on Newtonian principles. Every action has an equal reaction, says Newton, and with visualization you are trying to create a reaction in the real world by making a picture in the imaginary world. You form a picture of how you want reality to be, and the act of doing so begins to create the reality in the material world. However, while Level One techniques are effective, they do not touch the depths of the two underlying levels. Understanding all three levels, and knowing the simple techniques for applying each one, gives you a tremendous edge in your ability to create a successful life.

In the twentieth century, an Einsteinian view began to emerge. This view did not invalidate the essential wisdom of the Newtonian; rather, it added a new dimension to it. It is as if people prior to the twentieth century were seeing only height and width, when suddenly Einstein added depth to the picture and pointed out the space in which the picture was occurring.

Now, as the twenty-first century dawns, new depths are being added to both the Newtonian and Einsteinian views. I refer to this new paradigm as the Third Way, because there is no single word that accurately describes it.

Let's look at each of these in more depth.

Level One of Manifesting: The Newtonian

The Newtonian level draws on a simple fact of life and mind: for every action there is an equal reaction. If you roll a cue ball across the table and strike another ball, that ball will react in some way. In the same way, if you hold the belief that people cannot be trusted, you will likely produce that result for yourself. The belief will create the reaction of bringing untrustworthy people into your life and causing you to project mistrust onto people who might be completely trustworthy.

Usually it is our childhood programming that instills an issue such as "lack of trust" in our lives. Most of us don't wake up some morning and consciously choose mistrust: "I think I'm going to go around from now on looking suspiciously at people." These ideas are formed in vulnerable and powerless times in our lives, often before we can walk.

In Level One manifestation, you correct these old limitations by inserting consciously chosen positive words or imagery into your stream of thought. For example, you might notice yourself running a flurry of worry thoughts about money. As soon as you notice the worry thoughts passing through your mind, you let go of the worry and focus your attention on pictures of yourself being happy and successful and prosperous. This technique works miracles; I use it myself and have taught it to thousands of people. It is particularly useful for creating things in the material world. You can get a lot more done by focusing on positive actions you can take, rather than obsessing over what you don't have.

You can read about techniques like visualization and positive thinking in the works of William James and Ralph Waldo Emerson. In fact, James said that the greatest discovery of his time was that one could change the outer circumstances of one's life by changing one's thoughts. This is the Level One technique in its simplest form. If you are reading this book, I'll bet you have used a Newtonian technique sometime in your past. You have had the thought "How would I like my life to be?" which then began to create a new flow of possibilities based on your desires rather than your programming. You created a pattern in your mind, and it became manifest in your life.

Many of the most successful books on manifestation, from Napoleon Hill's *Think and Grow Rich* to Shakti Gawain's *Creative Visualization,* are based on Newtonian principles. For example, the core technique of Napoleon Hill is positive thinking: defining your goals and directing your mental energies into those goals. For many people, this is a crucial step forward, because they do not know what their goals are and are languishing in confusion or bitterness as a result. Unless we carry positive pictures of our goals in our minds we are likely to be held sway by negative ones.

Level Two: The Einsteinian

One of Einstein's great contributions was to describe the shift from the mechanistic view of Newton—a universe of moving parts pushing and pulling on one another—to a relativistic world in which consciousness plays a powerful role. I use an example originally attributed to Einstein to describe the new paradigm. Think about how you perceive time. Two minutes sitting on a hot stove feels like two hours; two hours with your beloved feels like two minutes. When we are contracting our consciousness (in pain or fear or boredom), time slows to a crawl and our goals seem to manifest slowly if at all. When we are expanding our consciousness in love and awareness and gratitude, our goals seem to manifest quickly, as if by magic.

To use a practical example, suppose you are experiencing anxiety about a forthcoming public speaking event. You decide to use a conscious manifestation program to deal with it and make your speech a success. A Level One technique might have you repeat an affirmation—"I am an able public speaker"—or create a visual image of yourself being applauded vigorously at the end of your speech. You are consciously inserting a more positive idea into your stream of thought. This is fine, but it overlooks a powerful potential ally: your experience of the world right now.

In Level Two, you work directly with your experience as it is rather than trying to insert another experience on top of it. To deal with your public speaking discomfort, you focus your attention on the rattle and hum of the anxiety in your body. You aren't trying to substitute something else for it. You are simply being with it, learning from it. As you do this you realize that you got punished for speaking up one day in the eighth grade. You said something you thought was profound, and the other kids laughed at you. As you make this realization, the rattle settles down into a pleasant hum then changes to a delicious feeling of ease. Now your speech looks like an exciting adventure rather than something to be afraid of. You have changed your expectation, but not by imposing your will—your positive picture of reality—onto the situation; instead, you have taken the raw material of reality and transformed it at the vibrational level. You now see the world differently because you have changed your consciousness at its very source.

The great advantage of Level Two manifestation is that we do not have to create a positive picture of what we think a desired outcome might be. It is hard to do this effectively, because you are trying to create a positive future from a present that may be clouded by limitations from the past. A Newtonian way of creating a new relationship would be to run a singles ad with thirty-two desired qualities of a potential partner listed. An Einsteinian way would be to feel whatever vibration is occurring in your body (perhaps loneliness or an unhealed wound from the past) and embrace it with your consciousness. I use this example because this is precisely what one of my clients did. First she tried the list approach, going into great detail about what she was looking for. Then she consulted me when it turned out disastrously.

She was trying to use a Newtonian approach when a Level Two technique was called for. Rather than have her do affirmations or create visualizations, I invited her to feel and love all the different emotions she felt about not having a close relationship. She began to work on shifting her state of consciousness about her aloneness. As she put it, "As soon as I learned to love myself for being alone, the phone started ringing and I met the man I'm dating now."

The reason this works is that sometimes Newtonian techniques like visualization can be a subtle way of ignoring things that need to be addressed. There may be unloved or unaccepted aspects of you that need to be embraced. If you repeat an affirmation that you are a good public speaker, you might not get to resolve the pain of an event that is still vibrating in your body years later.

The Third Way

The deepest level of manifestation is when your ideal life unfolds before you spontaneously with no Newtonian moves like visualization or Einsteinian moves like shifting your consciousness. You are completely at ease in the universe so that you move through it as if you belong there. You are in the right place at the right time; the universe itself seems to support you in your full expression. We usually need to master the Newtonian level before we can fully appreciate the Einsteinian. The Third Way requires a great deal of polish, practice, and vigilance in order to navigate and stay in harmony with it.

At first the Third Way opens in ways that may seem trivial but are actually signposts that one is moving in the correct direction. For me it opened with several realizations, what I now call stepping-stones to the Third Way. The central stepping-stone is a body feeling of letting go of the expectation of things' working a certain way and slipping into a benign openness to possibility. To understand what I mean, feel the difference inside yourself. As an experiment, adopt the body feeling of expectation that you will have potatoes for dinner. Then, let that go and adopt the body feeling of being completely open to all possibilities of what to have for dinner. The person who wishes to travel the Third Way must learn how to be nimble in letting go of the expectation and embracing openness to creative possibilities.

Just after I grasped the value of this shift in consciousness, I had an opportunity to use it in a manner that at first seemed trivial. Later, I saw that it was a sign of what would become possible as I got comfortable in the Third Way.

I was carrying a large box toward a door that led to a suite where my office was located. About fifty feet from the door, I had the thought that I wouldn't be able to get my keys out of my pocket and open the door without setting down the heavy box. Then, I realized something even worse: I had forgotten my office keys. It was late at night, and I saw no way I could unlock the main door or my office door. The building seemed deserted. I felt a wave of irritation at myself.

Remembering my new Third Way learning, though, I paused with the box and took a deep breath and let it go. I let go of the expectation that I had to get into my office. I stood still for about ten seconds, deep-breathing and relaxing my body.

Just then, one of my colleagues opened the door from the other side and saw me with the box. He held the door for me while I came in. My thought was that I would leave my box in the hall outside my office, where I was sure it would be safe. "Working late," my colleague said with a rueful shake of the head. He dashed off without a further glance.

Now inside the door, I looked down the hall toward my office. Standing near my office was the only security guard on campus whose first name I knew. He was obviously on his nightly door-checking rounds. "Hi, Jerry," I said. "How 'bout opening my office for me?" "Sure thing, Doc," he said, whipping out his master keys. A few seconds later and I was in my office, feeling most at home in the universe. The Third Way is when things are working miraculously well even when your conscious mind says otherwise.

You've no doubt had days like that; most of us have. But what I discovered is how to make them happen reliably and how to get back into the groove again when we drift out of the Third Way.

When you use Newtonian manifestation, you think up how you'd like your life to be, then you beam your chosen goals into the future with the power of your mind.

When you use Einsteinian manifestation, you love and appreciate things the way they are. The act of loving them transforms them, and you begin to move in a direction that will bring you more of what you want and need in your life.

In the Third Way you let go of pushing with your will and open to being supported effortlessly by the universe. You relax into your organic union with all creation, and by acknowledging your connection with infinite creation and infinite abundance, you allow yourself to be always in the right place at the right time for your maximum unfoldment to take place. This is the Third Way.

The art of the Third Way involves this initial shift followed by benign vigilance to notice when you start pushing too hard again. There is always a tendency to drift back into effortful push, which slows down the process of manifestation. When you notice you are pushing, the art is to slip back into the feeling of union with the universe and its infinite abundance. Later, I will describe a particular way of cultivating the Third Way when we explore the Master Technique for gaining access to it.

At this stage of my evolution, I can see twelve laws that are operating in the background of the Third Way. As I grew more familiar with them, I found myself living for longer periods of time in the magical world of the Third Way.

The Twelve Laws of the Third Way

I've taught and studied manifestation for over thirty years, so I've had the opportunity to watch thousands of people interact with the principles we're discussing. Certain concepts have emerged so clearly useful and reliable that I do not hesitate to call them laws. If a person stands up to lecture and argues that gravity is not a law, all I have to do is ask the person to jump and notice if he or she comes back down. I feel the same way about the Twelve Laws. Don't argue about whether they're laws or not until you've tried them out with sincere intent. I have, and they satisfy all my requirements of laws.

The Law of Unconscious Attraction

We attract by default those life experiences that are appropriate to our unconscious programming. Further, we tend to see those life experiences as ordained—"that's just the way life is"—rather than products of our conditioning that can be changed by conscious design. For example, if you have just enough cash each month to make ends meet, the Law of Unconscious Attraction explains that it's because you have an unconscious rule that requires life to show up that way for you. When I first saw this law at work at my own life, I was dumbfounded. It seemed so obvious. Why hadn't someone pointed this idea out to me in elementary school? Since then I have collected hundreds of examples of how people have changed these unconscious rules and by so doing changed the outer circumstances of their lives.

The Law of Conscious Creation

It is possible to introduce positive concepts and pictures into our minds consciously, and these positive mental ideas will change the outer circumstances of life. To continue the previous example (just having enough cash to get through the month), the Law of Conscious Creation invites you to drop a new thought into the stream. Make up a positive new idea, such as "I have plenty of money to do everything I want to do." Think it a few times until it feels comfortable, then sit back to watch the results. I have often been surprised at how quickly the new idea produced positive results.

This is the principle on which affirmations and visualizations work. If this is done skillfully, it produces positive results. Many people, however, get into trouble with this principle, not because it doesn't work, but because it works quite rapidly. However, the first thing it does is usually stir up a stronger version of the belief you are trying to replace.

For example, if you are using visualization for weight loss, your mental imagery of a slim body will often release powerful cravings for forbidden foods. More than one visualizer has gone on a binge through being unfamiliar with this problem.

I teach people how to use that power in the following way. In my manifestation work, I use affirmations and visualizations not so much as treatments in themselves, but as probes to stir up and reveal the negative programming. I might have the dieter use a visualization of himself living in a slim body. I ask him to focus on this image once a minute for ten minutes during our session, while I monitor and take notes on the various resistances that arise. By doing this, we bring up the things that would later sabotage the project if they surfaced by surprise.

The Law of Purpose

Your manifestation will ultimately be successful and satisfying to the extent it is in harmony with your overall life purpose. About twenty-five years ago, someone asked me what the chosen purpose of my life was. I stammered out something vague, but the truth was I didn't know. I had never sat down and figured out what my purpose was on this planet and what I intended to accomplish or experience. So I decided to find out. I went back to my apartment and sat down on the floor. I simply started asking myself the questions, "What is the purpose of my life? What am I really here to do?" Over the next hour I went through hell and heaven. First, the questions opened up a great deal of pain in me, because they revealed how many times I had acted out of the mere need to survive. I had done things I wouldn't have done consciously had I not been in the grip of some old survival issue. For example, I think I married my first wife purely out of a deep fear of being alone. My grandmother had just died, and I felt totally alone in the world. Along came a woman with a house and a car and social status. I got aboard without loving her or really even liking her at a fundamental level. Had I known about therapy in those days, I probably could have dealt with my grandmother's death in an hour of skilled treatment rather than avoiding it through four years of a mismatched marriage.

Often, a deep inquiry into purpose will yield powerful therapeutic information. Particularly, such an inquiry will often reveal cross-purposes that interfere with finding and expressing one's true and singular purpose. For example, many people were conceived for a certain purpose of their parents. One man I'm thinking of was conceived to replace his older brother who had died tragically. In his adult life he had to do a great deal of excavation to get beyond this purpose to one of his own choosing.

Sitting on the floor of my apartment, I finally got to a state of clarity and acceptance of the past. Okay, I thought; that was then and this is now. What is my purpose now? As I sat with the question hovering in my mind, a feeling of purpose began to appear in my body, almost like a piece of film developing into a recognizable image. I stayed with the feeling until it turned into words. The words were something like this: "I expand in love and creativity every day, as I work with others to help them expand in love and creativity." I tried the idea on, and it felt right in my body. I said it over a dozen times, then probably fifty more. Each time it shifted slightly, or the wording changed, but it was the same basic idea. Even though I have continued to ask myself about my purpose over the years, it has varied only slightly in wording since I discovered it. The basic feeling behind it has become a permanent backdrop of my life.

This is the value of the law of purpose: once you know what you are really about, you have a benchmark against which you can evaluate any life goal or activity. Suppose you have a decision to make about changing jobs. You can ask, "Is this new job in harmony with my purpose?" If you are honest with yourself, you will get valuable information each time you ask yourself a purpose question.

The Law of Personal Responsibility

Manifestation is enhanced by a special type of healthy responsibility. Unhealthy responsibility always takes less or more than 100 percent. If you take less than 100 percent, you are occupying the position of victim with regard to other people and the universe. If you take more than 100 percent, you are setting yourself up for burden and martyrdom. For a given manifestation project to work, you have to get the responsibility formula right, an elegant dance of taking complete responsibility while letting go of control. You have to take 100 percent responsibility yourself, while leaving 100 percent for the creative powers of the universe itself to work for you. In that way you develop a completely cocreative partnership with the universe around you. You work for it, and it works for you.

The Law of Pure Consciousness

Your experience in this moment is occurring in a field of consciousness, just as mine is. We can look up at the stars at night or the sky in the daytime and see at a glance that everything is occurring in a field of space. We can imagine, then, that the whole of creation is structured in a field of space, or pure consciousness. The ancient yogis called this field of space *akasha,* a word in Sanskrit that is filled—beginning, middle, and end—with the letter *a* ("Ah"), their term for the creative powers of the universe. In their cosmology, the universe originally and ultimately is engaged in a continual process of creation, carried out in a spirit of play symbolized by the sound of "Ah." The practical value of this law is this: unless our manifestation projects are filled with space, creation, and a sense of play, we will ultimately sabotage them by getting too attached to the outcome. As attachment increases, play ceases and freedom decreases. Then we will find a way to mess up the game so we can try again.

Later I will show you a process that allows you to gain access to space and pure consciousness directly. A specific type of question is also an effective way of finding space. For example, a person may have a life goal of amassing a large fortune. A question may be constructed that has a spacious quality to it. By "spacious quality" I mean that the question must be asked with genuine wonder, not with any attitude or expectation attached. Such a question might be, "How can I effortlessly amass a fortune of ten million dollars while fulfilling my life purpose?" If the question is big enough and you ask it sincerely, it will create more space in your experience. When you ask it, your normal mental processes will cease, opening a space for something new to occur. In that open space, which the philosopher J. Krishnamurti called "freedom from the known," there is room for miracles to occur. In one of Einstein's writings I read that he lived with a certain question for twenty-seven years before it developed into a coherent set of concepts. This was clearly a man who was comfortable stretching out into the spacious zone of the unknown.

The Law of Intention

We are always manifesting according to our intentions. In other words, we are always getting what we want. The problem is that until we choose consciously, our intentions are often unconscious and very limited. Part of the art of manifestation is learning how to see what our unconscious intentions are and choosing new intentions that fit our life purpose and chosen goals.

Once you learn this law, life becomes much simpler. I know mine did the moment I fully comprehended it. And I remember that exact moment. I was attending a series of lectures by Krishnamurti in the early seventies. In one of the talks, someone asked him what he thought of therapy. He said it was unnecessary if you knew one key fact of life: you don't need to look inside yourself for your unconscious; it can be seen readily on the outside by the results you produce. If you oversleep, assume you had an unconscious intention to oversleep. If you are single, don't burden yourself with claiming that your real intention is to be married. This sets up a conflict in yourself and delays you from asking a key question such as, "What's the lesson I need to learn from being single?"

This law is key to the manifestation process in general. The moment you initiate a manifestation project, you will flush to the surface your unconscious programming, one element of which is your unconscious intentions. I worked with a client awhile back who wants to write a book. He made a fortune in another line of work, but now he wants to put his philosophies into print. As he began the process of writing, he had wave after wave of anxiety appear in his body, accompanied by some disruptions in his family life. He put the book on hold as a result.

I invited him to look at all these things as natural parts of the process of manifesting a book. You initiate a positive, new version of yourself, move through a flurry of internal and external stuff that's in the way, and if you move through it successfully, you have a finished product. I invited him to try on the idea, "I have an unconscious intention to try but fail to write a book." At first he argued that this was inaccurate. "You don't understand," he said. "I really want to write a book." "The conscious part of you does," I said, "but let's assume that your unconscious may feel otherwise." It didn't take him long to make his breakthrough. His body language shifted dramatically the moment he accepted that the unconscious result he was trying to produce was "no book." Then we could begin to work on why he might not want to produce a book.

There were some of the usual psychological reasons. For one, he had been told by a variety of authority figures when he was young that he was uncreative, and he was still in thrall to these old programs. But the big reason was that he had never failed in his other career; he had enjoyed twenty-five years of rousing success. Suddenly he had invented a new game for himself, one in which he could potentially and publicly fail. This fear gripped him visibly as we broke through to it. After he had worked with it for a while, though, a smile brightened his face. "So what?" he said. That is an excellent attitude to have toward failure, and with it he returned to his manuscript. The ultimate proof came a year down the line, when I saw a stack of his books on the "New Releases" table of my neighborhood bookstore.

The Law of Completion

Human beings have an innate drive toward completion. Incompletion haunts us. Completion is organic to life; leaves turn green in the spring, golden in the autumn, then drop to the ground in winter. Human beings have the same cycles of completion, and if we honor them we feel in harmony with ourselves. However, we have found ways to interfere with our natural cycles in dozens of different ways. Some of these ways are beneficial, but others are disastrous for us and our later manifestation efforts. Attention to completion is a crucial element of the manifestation process.

Here's how it works. If we leave a situation incomplete in some way, it consumes energy, much like an electrical circuit that is left open. Some specific incompletions consume the most energy:

Promises made and not kept
Actions you feel guilty about
Important unspoken communications
Significant regrets and resentments

The big problem with incompletions is they eat up the very energy needed for conscious, creative manifestation. The act of completing them—even making a tiny conscious step toward completing them—opens the gate to a great deal more energy flow through your life. When I teach classes in manifestation, we give a great deal of attention to handling incompletions large and small. Often, in fact, taking care of a few significant incompletions is the only thing a person needs to do to get a positive flow of manifestation going.

The Law of Authenticity

Honesty with ourselves and with others creates a positive field around us that attracts harmonious manifestations. Dishonesty creates a negative force field that eventually sabotages our manifestation projects or interferes with our ability to enjoy them. What I have noticed from working with many clients is that manifestation is often slowed to a crawl by any act of inauthenticity. Many times I have watched with awe as people got their success and happiness flowing again by telling some long-withheld truth or handling an agreement they had made and forgotten.

The Law of Clear Request

Asking—simply making a request—is one of the most powerful manifestation techniques available to us. However, many barriers, internal and external, must be cleared up in order to ask for things effectively. The apostle Paul was among the first people in written history to deal with this law. In his letter to the Philippians, he counseled them to deal with their anxiety by clearly asking for what they wanted. Whether we are asking God or the neighbor next door, most of us have a difficult time making requests. Our requests are often laden with heavy emotional baggage like fear or anger so that the request gets lost in the noise of the unspoken feelings. For example, I have spent the better part of several therapy hours helping a couple learn to ask for what they wanted from each other in bed. In order to make a simple request— "I'd like you to initiate sex sometimes"—they often had to go down through layers of anger, despair, entitlement, resignation, and fear of rejection. This is not surprising, though, given how little positive coaching we receive in our families of origin on the key life skill of asking for what we want. In some families, asking for what you want is ridiculed, scorned, and punished.

The Law of Creative Expression

Our manifestations will bear fruit and bring satisfaction to the extent that they represent us at our full creative expression. When you hold back from a commitment to full expression, you will feel unrewarded no matter how materially successful you are. In working with entertainers, for example, I have seen this problem close-up. One of my clients released an album that sold a million copies but was motivated by wanting to cash in on her success. She felt empty as a result. By contrast, an earlier album, even though it did not do as well commercially, still fills her with pride because she put everything she had into it. There is a part of us that knows clearly and registers dissatisfaction when we are just going through the motions.

Full creative expression is the answer to many of life's ills. Many people languish in unfulfilling jobs and other life situations because they have not made a full-scale commitment to their creative expression. One of the central questions I ask people as they create manifestation projects is "Does this represent the most expanded version of yourself?" As we move toward a "Yes!" I can see the light begin to shine from their eyes.

The Law of Love

Only manifestation that comes from a clear place of love ultimately feels satisfying. Visions created and launched out of fear prove unsatisfactory and often disastrous for those involved.

Love is the ultimate healer, and it comes into play in manifestation in the following way. Often the act of envisioning a goal brings to the surface issues that only love can embrace. For example, let's say you set in motion a manifestation process designed to increase your income threefold. The first thing that may occur is that threefold fears get stirred up. This may be the very issue that has been keeping you at your old level of income. In other words, you may be limiting yourself because you have not been willing to challenge the fear of living in an expanded version of yourself. Naturally, as the manifestation process kicks in, you will have to go through the gate of that fear in order to stabilize at the new, higher level. Sometimes love is the only way through that gate.

I remember a panicked predawn call from a man on the West Coast with whom I had done a phone consultation the day before. He was a businessman and philanthropist whom I had met at several social functions over the years. He scheduled an appointment to work on something that he described as his "final frontier." It turned out to be the issue of relationship. He had created wealth and a powerful social network, but he had never been in a loving relationship. Now in his late fifties, he wanted to find out what it felt like to love and be loved. I worked with him through the session on creating a set of affirmations and visualizations to bring a loving woman into his life. I also prepped him carefully for what was likely to come up, namely, all his fears of intimacy, which had caused him to avoid a close relationship all his life. But I woefully underestimated their intensity.

In the still-dark hours of the next morning, I received a call from him, hyperventilating and babbling. Through coaching him in a few minutes of conscious breathing, I got him settled down enough to tell me what had happened. After our session he had felt fine until midnight, but as he was trying to get to sleep he awakened all the fears he had been repressing all his life. Afraid to call me, he spent the night—five hours!—pacing up and down the stretch of beach in front of his house. By the time he called me, things had gotten to a crisis point. He felt he was going crazy.

Love saved the day. I asked him to stop in his tracks and love himself for being scared. He had a flurry of resistance to this idea. He had been a fighter pilot in the Second World War and a pilot ever since. "If I ever let myself admit I'm scared, I'm not sure I would be able to function" was the way he put it. "I've gotten where I am by never being scared." I told him there was a major fallacy in this way of thinking.

I pointed out that by the time his mind got around to denying he was scared, his body had already been scared for quite a while. It had probably always been scared. Pretending he wasn't scared was just a coping tool, one of many and by no means the best. Denial exists to get you through a crisis, not to get you healthy. I told him, "If you want to get the fear out of your body, you have to accept that you're scared and love yourself for being that way." He took a deep, shuddering breath and did it.

Within ten seconds everything had changed. When he got words again, he told me that the fear turned to pure sensation then to a feeling of exhilaration as he loved it directly. I had seen this happen many times, so it didn't surprise me. For him the shift was a revelation. It was the first time he could recall feeling the power of love. "Now you know it's real," I said. "Would you be willing to feel it all the time in your life?" In a moment of wondrous vulnerability, he said yes.

The happy ending to the story was that he befriended a very warm woman a month or two later. I lost touch with them a few years later. This event sticks in my mind because few times does a therapist get the luxury of bearing witness to the precise moment a key issue shifts for a client. Often the shift may be precipitated by something during the session, but the change occurs during the other 167 hours of the week. Here, though, was a living, breathing example of the power of love to heal a lifetime of pain and create an open space in which a relationship could be born.

The Law of Gratitude

As we progress along the path of conscious manifestation, we can learn to lead with the heart. What I mean by this is that we can learn to walk through life with an "always, already" feeling of gratitude for life itself.

Gratitude is a powerful tool for manifestation. A field of gratitude around us clears a positive path through life in which every step we take is in the right direction. A great deal of work must often be done on ourselves before we can greet every moment of life with a grateful heart. Until then, we may rise in gratitude for a while, then bring ourselves down by a challenge. If we handle it successfully, gratitude may come to the fore again to lead the way.

A key insight that opens the heart is to regard all of life's experiences as learning opportunities, as challenges to love some part of yourself that most needs acceptance. Some people greet life's events with an attitude that guarantees misery: "I refuse to accept that this is happening to me, and I will not rest until I find out who is at fault here." A major shift happens when we drop this attitude in favor of another: "I acknowledge that this is happening, and I open myself to learning all the lessons I can harvest from this experience." The former attitude is one of cosmic ungratefulness, while the latter is one of heart-opening wonder to the mysteries of life itself.

The Techniques of Manifestation

Now let's focus on how-to. There are three master techniques, each designed to reflect one of the three levels of manifestation.

The Master Technique for Newtonian Manifestation

The master technique first involves developing a clear, centered state of consciousness. To launch a new vision, it helps to have a relaxed body and an open mind. If you try to create a new vision when you're tense or off center, you may unconsciously attach these qualities to the vision.

So be willing to center yourself as you begin. I use a very simple process, one that almost everyone can learn to do easily.

Sit comfortably, eyes open or closed. Take slow, deep belly breaths. Breathe comfortably all the way in, then just as comfortably all the way out. If you have a second hand, time a few breaths to get them slow and easy. If you take complete breaths of eight to ten seconds, you will likely feel centered in less than five minutes. In other words, breathe in for four to five seconds, then breathe out for four to five seconds.

When a relaxed, open state is attained, then create present-tense sentences and moving pictures that represent your desire. For example, you might say to yourself, "I sell my house for a profit of $75,000," as you visualize a happy family playing a board game in the house you're trying to sell. After saying the sentences and seeing the pictures a few times, return to the clear, centered space. It takes only a few minutes. I've found it's best to do it a few minutes every day, as opposed to once a week for an hour.

The Master Technique for Einsteinian Manifestation

Rather than using conscious powers of the mind, the Level Two technique invokes powers of the heart. Using the searchlight of your consciousness, you locate aspects of yourself and the world that are difficult to love. As those aspects of ourselves and the people around us are loved and accepted, an open space of heart-sweetened gratitude begins to emerge. Once this state is attained, the work is done.

1. Begin with a body map. Draw a whole-body picture of yourself. A simple sketch will do just fine. Indicate the parts of your physical body you have difficulty loving. For one person it might be the nose, for another the belly. Draw arrows or shade in those areas that are difficult to love.

Then make a feeling map. Begin by locating the three most troublesome feelings—fear, anger, sadness—on your body map. Therapists call these the Big Three, because they give people the biggest challenge. Most people feel fear in their stomachs, sadness in their chests, anger in their neck, shoulders, and jaws. However, everyone has their own particular locations for their feelings. Indicate with arrows or shade in the places in your body where your Big Three feelings reside.

2. Next, pick other feelings with which you struggle: boredom, sexual desire, mania. After you have finished entering feelings on your map, indicate the mental thoughts that give you the biggest challenge. Here are some that people struggle with:

Jealousy
Envy
Competitiveness
Comparativeness
Ruminating about the past
Fantasizing about the future
Obsessing

List any thoughts that bother you up near the head of your body map.

When your map is complete, you should have a graphic representation of those feelings, thoughts, and body aspects that you have difficulty loving.

3. Make a commitment to loving those aspects of yourself. You can feel the commitment in your body, or you can say a sentence: "I commit to loving all aspects of myself." It may take you a minute or a year to have the actual experience of loving those aspects of yourself—after all, you have spent a lifetime wrestling with them—but the important step is the first one: making a commitment.

Now go through each unloved item on your map, completing the following sentence:

I commit to loving my ______________________________.

Example: I commit to loving my anger.
I commit to loving my nose.
I commit to loving my jealousy.

Remember, the commitment to learning to love "the way things are" is the first step to loving them the way they are. The moment you love things the way they are, they are not the way they were any longer. Now they've been bathed in love.

4. Generate the feeling of love inside yourself. Do it however you can. If you can readily feel love, go ahead and put your attention on it. If it's slow to come, you can jump-start yourself by thinking of someone you love a lot, then feeling the love in your body. Another way is to think of some activity or place you love—riding your horse or walking your favorite stretch of beach—and then feel the quality of love connected with that activity or place. Many people experience love as an expanding glow of warmth and

acceptance in the heart region. Your love may feel like that or some entirely different way. Just feel as much love as you can. Remember, your commitment and intention are as important as the feelings themselves.

Go through each item you listed earlier. Focus your attention on each item—anger, nose, jealousy—and feel love for each one. Rest your attention lightly on the item, love it, then move on to the next item. All you need to do is touch each unloved aspect of yourself with love, and this action opens the gateway to a new type of effortless manifestation in your life.

The Master Technique for Third-Way Manifestation

By its very nature, the Third Way cannot be pursued. Instead of chasing it, you relax and open to it, then enjoy it when it unfolds. Grasping for it definitely chases it away. I recommend opening to it by embracing the following concepts. Embrace them in your mind first, then feel them in your body. Then let them go. The sequence is: think . . . feel . . . let go. Keep it easy, keep it simple, and definitely don't push.

Begin by thinking this thought: "I open to my full evolution, and I let go of my expectations that my life has to be any particular way." Think the thought, then feel a letting go of expectation in your body. Let go, and take life as it comes. Let go, and let things be the way they are. Relax your requirement for them to be a certain way. Become willing to be surprised by the magnificent unfolding of your evolution.

Now think another thought: "I am connected to infinite creation and infinite abundance." Shift into your body, and feel your connection with infinite creation and infinite abundance. Feel how your whole being is an infinite, abundant creation. Feel your connection with the universe, how you are a part of all that is, a living and breathing connection with infinite creation and infinite abundance.

Now think another thought: "I reach my goals by relaxing into the support that is around me all the time. I get to where I want to go by letting myself be supported and carried along on a lifestream of support that is around me all the time." Feel yourself relax into being supported. Let go of the I-have-to-do-it-all-myself mentality, and feel your body relax into being supported.

Now think another thought: "I honor and appreciate the support I am constantly being given." Feel in your body the sense of honoring the support you're being given all the time in your life. Feel appreciation for the hundreds of people who are supporting you every day: the person who paints the stripes on the freeway, the person who washes your cup in the restaurant, the baggage handlers and pilots and family members and co-workers who help make your life work. Honor and appreciate them right this moment, feeling the appreciation in your body as you think about honoring them in your mind.

Rest and relax for a moment before returning to your usual activities.

The Third Way requires our willingness to be equals in the universe. If we are equal with all that is, we support the universe and the universe supports us. When we relax into the support that is happening all around us, we can be carried faster to our destination.

Imagine floating in a gentle stream on a summer day. If you are trying to steer through the stream, you don't enjoy the journey and you don't get there very fast. Just relax into the stream and find the center of it. It knows where it's going. It will flow around rocks rather than through the middle of them. It will take the path of least resistance and get there when it gets there. This is the Third Way.

I have seen all three levels of manifestation work miracles in many people's lives. There is a natural progression from one level to the next. In the beginning of your journey of conscious living, you will probably work (as I did) for a long time on the simple act of shifting from negative thinking ("Why doesn't anybody love me?") to positive ("What could I do right now to open myself more to love in my life?"). In Level One, we begin to feel the power of thinking about what we want, rather than obsessing about what we don't, and moving consciously toward our goals. As we gradually reorient ourselves in a more positive direction, we will inevitably hit barriers in the world and in the depths of ourselves. It is then time for Level Two, where we embrace all of ourselves in loving acceptance. Ultimately, with enough loving excursions into the hurt places in ourselves and others, we will begin to experience life as a flowing journey. We gradually learn to feel our way into being in the right place at the right time. This is the Third Way, in which we will be guided from one fine experience to the next.

Please understand that this progression is not linear and that the art of manifestation is far from an exact science. Manifestation is best approached as an experiment and as an adventure. However, I have watched the progression unfold magically in my own life and in the lives of many others. In the beginning, when it works only in fits and starts, I predict you will find the adventure interesting at the very least. As you grow more skilled, I can virtually guarantee that you will come to call your progress sublime.

Closing

One Breath at a Time

Here we end our journey together. Now you know everything I know about conscious living. My intention was to share all I've learned. I can think of nothing I've held back. I plan to continue along my journey of wonder wherever my questing spirit takes me, and I imagine you plan to do the same. For all of us the journey proceeds one step at a time, and the path of conscious living opens before us one breath at a time. The beauty of conscious living is that it requires no teachers save a willing heart and a wondering mind. Every time I've opened my heart or my mind—every time I've taken that next conscious breath—I've been showered with more blessings than I ever dreamed of.

I believe that all the lessons of conscious living are free for the asking and wondering. In other words, we know it all deep inside us. Conscious living comes from awakening contact with the organic flow of the spirit inside us. Our troubles begin when we lose touch with the flow. Our troubles end when we remember to ask a conscious question, speak an authentic truth, take a conscious breath. Then we're back in the flow again, walking our path of wonder and insight, connecting with other sojourners.

Thank you for taking the time to walk and talk with me. The questing spirit in me salutes that spirit in you. Blessings on your journey.

About the Author

Gay Hendricks is the author of more than twenty books dealing with personal growth, relationships, and corporate transformation. After a twenty-five-year academic career at Stanford University and the University of Colorado, he founded the Hendricks Institute in Santa Barbara, California, which is codirected by his wife and creative partner, Dr. Kathlyn Hendricks.

Information about their books, tapes, and seminars on conscious living can be obtained by visiting their Web site:

http://www.hendricks.com